Patricia Hewitt

PRIVACY REPORT

National Council for Civil Liberties

Cover design by Public Voice Communications Ltd

Copyright   September 1977 National Council for Civil Liberties
ISBN 0 901108 68 5
Printed by Robendene Ltd, Chesham

Acknowledgements

I should like to thank Bill Birtles, Joe Hanlon, Ed Harriman, Trudy Hayden, Barry Hugill, Jo Jacobs, Marek Laskowski, Jim Michael, Bart Milner and Tony Smythe for their help with this report, and the thousands of people who have complained to NCCL about invasions of their privacy.

Contents

Introduction	1
Privacy and information	4
National government	11
Local government	23
Education	35
Medical records	39
Employment	52
The police and the security services	62
Cash, credit and computers	72
Privacy and the media	84
A programme for action	87

Introduction

This pamphlet is about your right to control personal information about yourself. The collection and use of information about someone — information which may be irrelevant, inaccurate or unlawfully obtained — creates an 'information prison' from which it is hard to escape. It is generally recognised that a person's criminal record may effectively imprison him, trapping him in unemployment and poor housing, long after he has served the sentence imposed. What most people don't realise is that everyone is, actually or potentially, trapped in an information prison, where the contents of a file can determine your chances of a job, a home or a credit agreement. A debt paid off years earlier, or never paid because the goods were faulty, may ruin your chances of getting goods on hire purchase or acquiring a credit card. More seriously, information about a criminal conviction years ago, an investigator's report based on malicious gossip, or speculation about your politics or your sex life may shut the doors to promotion or even to employment. The information prison has no bars, but the prison is all the more effective for its secrecy.

Here are some examples of people who have come to NCCL for help.

Mr C, attempting to expand a small, but profitable business, suddenly found himself unable to get credit. He went to the offices of a local trade association specialising in credit reports and asked for a reference on his own firm. The manager pulled out a record card and said: 'Don't deal with that bastard; he's a bad risk — people like him should be locked up.' Although the record stated that Mr C had been served with county court debt judgments over a period of three years, these judgments had in fact been made against Mr C's father, who had incurred them when he was ill and dying.

Mrs D wrote on behalf of her sister who had been told she couldn't buy a gas cooker on HP because her husband was paying a debt out of his wages under a county court judgment. 'My sister is very upset as she hasn't owed a penny in her life. She pays her rent and is not in arrears. The house is in her name; she pays £8 per week and never misses her furniture money.'

Carol P was a separated mother claiming supplementary benefits when she saw the file kept on her by the local office. The file contained the information she had given them, but also included comments and speculation about herself and her friends. It said that she was neurotic, regarded her husband as a 'father figure' and commented on her sexual relationship with her husband. The report speculated on her politics and her possible relationship with other men, including a man (described in detail) who had accompanied her to the office. The file even included the note she had left pinned to the door for a friend one day.

Geoffrey T has a number of convictions which made it difficult for him to get a job. But he is a reformed man and had no convictions for the previous five years, when he found himself charged with 'obtaining money by deception'. Mr T had got a job with British Rail, telling them that he had no previous convictions. He was taken on as a guard and worked satisfactorily for 18 months, when British Rail discovered his convictions. (Criminal records are supposed to be confidential: as we show on page 62, they often aren't.) He was then suspended and prosecuted for obtaining the wages he had earned in the last year and a half. At his trial, the manager of his depot said he was an exemplary employee, honest, loyal and hardworking. Mr T sued British Rail for unfair dismissal. Although he lost his case, the union took it up and he is now back with British Rail, being retrained for the job he used to do.

Mr I had been employed as a security guard for 2½ years when he resigned, fed up with the extent of petty theft in the firm. Although the personnel manager said that he would get good references, he was dismissed from his next job after two months, because his references were inadequate. He managed to get a copy of the reference, which accused him of misconduct and incompetence. Mr I's solicitors advised an action for libel. But there is no legal aid for libel, and Mr I did not have the £100 which the solicitors wanted to start the action.

An NSPCC inspector called one evening when Mr M was out, and asked Mrs M if he could see their baby daughter. When Mr M returned and found out what had happened, he phoned the inspector, who said he was investigating allegations of baby-battering. The M's couldn't find out why they were suspected, or what would happen. So Mr M had a look at the file on them in the health visitor's brief case, and discovered that their child had been placed on the 'at risk' register. The M's still don't know why they are on the register and say they have never hurt their child. Mrs M is terrified that the baby will be taken away from them; Mr M is threatening to refuse to let any official see the child, so that the local authority will be forced to go to court and give evidence for their suspicions.

The right to privacy

Misuse of personal information is an invasion of individual privacy. Everyone needs to be alone sometimes and people have a right to keep their private lives and beliefs free from interference or intrusion, and to expect that their correspondence and private conversations will not be eavesdropped and that their home will not be invaded. Part of this right to privacy is the right to control the information which is collected by others about you, and the use to which it is put.

Of course, privacy is not an absolute right. Any community will make legitimate demands of the individual, which involve a necessary infringement of privacy. But individual freedom and social responsibility are not mutually exclusive principles, although reconciling them may present difficulties. The community has, for instance, an interest in the collection of information on an individual's credit-worthiness, in order to minimise bad debts. But it also has an equal interest in ensuring the relevance and accuracy of such information, and making sure that the individual can control its use.

An American specialist in government secrecy and individual privacy has defined the importance of information privacy in this way:

> 'Power may come out of the barrel of a gun, but far more power comes out of a computer or databank, particularly if the information in it relates to people who do not know that it has been collected or cannot challenge its accuracy or use.... The definition of privacy as 'the right to control information about oneself' is therefore a good one. ....
> 'The widespread collection and use of personal information is, of course, an inevitable feature of our society. The social services we regard as essential — medical, legal, social welfare, educational, credit, insurance — can only be performed when there is full and honest disclosure by the persons served to those performing the service. Unfortunately, the service providers often fail to consider the larger forces of social control whose unwitting instruments they become when they collect data from their clients. We must, therefore, constantly guard against the use of personal information as a means of exercising social control by establishing procedures to ensure that, to the maximum possible extent, people can disclose what they want about themselves only to those whom they want to tell.'[1]

This pamphlet describes the history of the privacy campaign in Britain, and the dangers involved in uncontrolled information-gathering about individuals. It deals with the way information is collected and used by national government; local government; employers; credit reference agencies; the health service; schools and colleges; the police and the security services. We compare the lack of protection for individual privacy in this country with the position in other countries. And we set out a programme for legislation and administrative action which would protect your right to control information about you.

---

1) 'Privacy and Social Control', John Shattuck, Privacy Report, Vol III No 8, March 1976 (American Civil Liberties Union)

Privacy and information

The campaign for privacy

In 1968, as part of its contribution to International Human Rights Year, NCCL published *Privacy Under Attack*.[1] This report — the first comprehensive analysis of threats to privacy in the United Kingdom — concluded that 'the time for urgent action is *now*.'

In 1967, Alex Lyon MP introduced a Right of Privacy Bill, which was followed in 1969 by further Private Members' Bills to control data banks and to license private investigators. That year, NCCL published two draft Bills, one to provide for a general right of privacy, the other to control the collection of personal information. The second bill, which was introduced by Leslie Huckfield MP, would have established a Data Banks Tribunal to license and control the collection of information about individuals.

A Justice Report in 1970[2] recommended the creation of a general legal right to privacy, and Brian Walden MP introduced a Bill to give effect to this proposal. The Government persuaded Mr Walden to withdraw his Bill in return for the establishment of a Committee, chaired by Sir Kenneth Younger, to investigate invasions of privacy. At the end of that year, NCCL and the National Computing Centre Ltd organised a workshop conference on the data bank society, which brought together lawyers, computer technologists and those concerned with the problems of privacy raised by widespread computerisation of personal records.[3]

The Younger Committee, to which NCCL gave substantial evidence, reported in 1972. Although the Committee did not support the creation of a general right of privacy, it made a number of proposals to deal with specific problems. (Mr Lyon wrote a minority report, upholding a general right of privacy; in 1974, he became Minister of State at the Home Office but failed to convert the Government to his views.) The Younger Report was then shelved by the Government for over three years. The only step forward was the Consumer Credit Act 1974, which was not implemented until 1977, giving individuals the right to see and correct a file held on them by a credit reference agency. Further response to Younger waited until December 1975, when the Government published a White Paper on computers[4], committing it to the creation of a Data Protection Authority eventually. In the meantime, the Data Protection Committee was set up to prepare more detailed proposals for legislation.

The record of the last seven years, therefore, is one of almost total inaction. It is depressing to compare this with the progress made in the United States of America, particularly since Watergate made privacy a political priority. The Fair Credit Reporting Act of 1970 established limited rights for the subjects of credit reference files; the Privacy Act 1974 has given US citizens the right to see and challenge files held on them by federal agencies, including some personnel records on federal employees (but excluding national security and criminal investigation records); the amended Freedom of Information Act, 1966, has opened some FBI and CIA files to individual scrutiny; and a further Act gave students in schools and colleges the right to see and challenge their files. The Privacy Act also established a Privacy Protection Study Commission, which reported in July 1977, and a number of other privacy proposals have been placed before Congress in the last two years.

Data banks in the United Kingdom

Few people realise the scale on which personal information is collected in this country. A Government White Paper on government use of computerised data banks[5] revealed that at the end of 1975 there were 220 different functions carried out by central government which involve computerised personal information about identifiable individuals. They include records on teachers and school-leavers (Department of Education and Science); drivers' and vehicle licences (Department of the Environment); surveys of workers (Department of Employment); social security contribution records (Department of Health and Social Security); the police national computer (Home Office); tax records (Inland Revenue); the census (Office of Population, Censuses and Surveys); and National Health Service records. The White Paper list omits computerised personnel files on civil servants themselves, and also gives little information about the extent to which local authorities use computers.

Most computerised government data banks contain between 10,000 and 1 million names. Some are far larger: the Census covers the entire population and NHS records are almost as extensive. Local Authority records will eventually cover the entire population.

In addition, of course, there are the non-computerised data banks maintained by national government — including files kept on unemployed workers, and supplementary benefits claimants. As we argue later, manually-stored files can present as great a danger to the individual as a computerised system.

Data banks in the private sector include records on employees which, in large organisations, are increasingly likely to be computerised; the records of credit reference agencies, almost entirely manually-stored; bank records; the records of private detectives and security firms; market research files; sales information maintained by retail companies, mailing houses etc; and medical records held by insurance companies and private medical bodies. The National Computer Index, which in 1975 covered 13,263 computers in Britain, representing about 75% of the capital value of computer installations, listed in June 1975 over 2,000 computerised data banks which included personal information about individuals in the insurance, banking and finance sector of industry alone.[6]

You cannot avoid finding your way in to a databank. Your name will come up over and over again – in the Census; in health records; as a car-driver or owner; as an employee or self-employed person; as a national insurance contributor; as someone claiming benefit while ill, unemployed or retired; as someone with a criminal conviction or someone suspected of an offence; as a debtor or an applicant for credit; as a holder of a bank account; and so on.

What does it matter, all this information? There are four important ways in which data banks can threaten your privacy:

– the information on you may be collected unlawfully or by underhand methods, or without your knowledge or consent;
– your file may contain information which is inaccurate, incomplete, out of date or irrelevant;
– other people may be able to see information which you believed was stored in a confidential file;
– the information you gave for one purpose may be transferred, without your consent or even your knowledge, for an entirely different use.

A case-study of the operation of one credit reference agency illustrates these dangers vividly. In 1970, the directors of Tracing Services Ltd, an agency with records on millions of people, were convicted of conspiracy to effect a public mischief. Its employees had posed as doctors, police officers, tax inspectors and social security officers in order to obtain confidential information. As we explain on page 73, the law controlling the way in which information is gathered is entirely inadequate.

The accuracy and relevance of credit files is often dubious. One person may be confused with another of the same name; someone recently moved to a new address finds they are refused credit because of debts incurred by a previous tenant; gossip from neighbours or local tradespeople is used as a substitute for fact; or a debt is recorded, with no explanation that the debt remained unpaid because the goods bought were defective. The TSL files were index cards, containing brief information about the consumer and the name of the guarantor; in some cases, a scribbled note – 'left 6 months ago, leaving debts everywhere' – had been added to the back of the card, undated, unsigned and without supporting evidence. Since individuals had no right to see their credit reference files until 1977, there was no right for any of the millions of people held on TSL records to challenge the accuracy of their records.

In 1973, TSL went bankrupt. Early in 1975, its cards were put on the open market by a firm which had acquired some of its assets. These files – although in the end bought by NCCL, which destroyed them – could have been bought by any individual or organisation, however unscrupulous. Even while TSL remained active, anyone willing to pay the small fee could obtain information on an individual covered by their records. As the section on credit reference agencies shows, the new Consumer Credit Act goes only a small way towards dealing with the problems posed by credit reference operations.

Computerisation

The threat to individual privacy posed by data banks does not, in essence, change if the information is computerised instead of being stored in filing cabinets. Information may still be gathered unlawfully; it may still be wrong or irrelevant; it may still be misused or leaked to the wrong people. NCCL has criticised the Government for limiting its proposals on individual privacy to *computerised* data banks, leaving manually-stored records entirely uncontrolled.

But computerisation does change the scale of the problem. To take an example given to the Data Bank Society workshop in 1970, every time you stay at a hotel in the United Kingdom, your name and address should be entered in the register. It would be virtually impossible to trace your movements around the country as long as this involved inspecting every hotel register. But if the registers were computerised — with the hotel keeper able to transmit information to a central data bank — it would be very easy to prepare an 'inverted file', bringing together every entry with your name and address. Thus, the computer can 'reorganise a large quantity of information (each element of which is separately harmless) into a new quality of informaltion which may reveal more than the individual wishes to be known.'[7]

As records are computerised, it becomes possible to link separate systems, so that, for instance, government officials could have almost instant access to all the information now held separately on one individual — family relationships; previous and present addresses; criminal record; driving license and vehicle ownership records; social security records; income tax returns; medical treatment, including any history of mental ill-health; credit rating; social work reports; political or trade union activities and so on. According to a report prepared for the United States Senate Committee on Government Operations, the technical feasibility for linking several data systems and record compatibility and standardisation has been studied within the Home Office.[8] But the Government's White Paper denies that the Government has any plans to construct a central data bank: 'the administrative advantages to be gained from such a course are debatable and the practical difficulties and costs would be formidable — and they have no intention of allowing the computer systems under their control to be linked together to produce such a result.'[9] Legislative controls are needed to ensure that a future Government does not abuse the new technology in the name of efficiency or security.

In *The Assault on Privacy,* Professor Arthur Miller stresses the vulnerability of computerised data banks to espionage, eavesdropping and error.[10] The information itself may be wrongly programmed, because of an error by a programmer or a clerk transcribing information from, for instance, medical records. If the information is stored on magnetic tape, it is far more susceptible to theft, duplication or damage than a manual system (a single tape, containing information on thousands of people or the control programme for an entire system, could be copied or wiped out in minutes). If the information is stored in the central processor of a 'time share' system (where a number of users can plug into the system simultaneously) there is a danger of electronic 'crossed lines' where part of one user's information is made available to the next. The control programme for the system itself is vulnerable to intrusion or alteration: a spy who gets access to the control programme can allow unauthorised people to take information from the system, or feed inaccurate information into it.

There are numerous examples of the computer frauds which have been carried out by enterprising operators.[11] At Massachusetts Institute of Technology, Professor Miller reports, students in a computer-assisted teaching programme tapped computers handling classified national defence information. At the University of Michigan, students deciphered the access codes to the university computer system, which had remote terminal points throughout the campus, and destroyed a number of files. 'Phone phreaks' succeeded in tapping the U.S. internal phone system, allowing them to get access to computer terminals using telephone lines to relay information. John Draper, later sent to prison for his activities, tapped the FBI's data bank which holds records of everyone arrested or investigated by the Bureau and even succeeded in getting access to the military's top 'secret' phone system. In 1974, a 15-year-old English schoolboy, using a teletype terminal in his school, cracked the secret codes of a time-sharing system, gaining access to the most secret files of other users of the system and discovering how to change the passwords, cut off other users and even alter the bills that customers would have to pay.[12]

Nonetheless, the use of the computer itself to protect privacy is vital. The Government White Paper stresses that the computer 'can be programmed so as to limit access to certain data, or to require the use of a special password, or knowledge of a secret code, before the system can be entered. It can be programmed so that certain operations are forbidden and the system gives an alarm if anyone attempts to carry them out. It can also be programmed to provide audit information, logging all operations — or operations of certain kinds — for subsequent inspection.'[13]

Even security measures of this kind are, however, vulnerable to the computer operators themselves. An operator could alter the main programme to allow unauthorised people to bypass protective devices, or could simply tell unauthorised people what codes or passwords were needed to get access to the system. Programmers may subvert a system for money or out of curiosity or spite; they may exchange information from colleagues from other systems; they may want to help the police or some other agency; they may simply want to prove that they can do it. The larger the number of people employed in computerised systems, the more likely it is that an unauthorised agency will bribe an operator, or introduce its own operator, in order to gain access to information.

The vulnerability of computer security vividly displayed in charges brought against a United States organisation, the Factual Service Bureau, which had obtained personal information illegally from the FBI's National

Crime Information Centre, the Social Security Administration and the tax returns of the Internal Revenue. The investigators used only a telephone, posing as police officers, or paying federal employees to get the information. The data banks which FSB cracked were some of the most secret held by the United States Government.[14]

Computerised data banks are increasingly likely to use an 'on line' system, with remote terminals, such as the small TV screens on top of a keyboard used for airline bookings, which allow the operator to type in instructions or information and read information back off the screen. An 'on line' system can provide information from the central store within a few seconds to a terminal hundreds of miles away. The Police Computer, for instance, provides hundreds of remote terminals for use by local police forces. By increasing the number of people who can put information into a system and take information out, remote terminals increase the danger that an unauthorised user will break the access code or forge the necessary identification, or that an authorised user will alter the protection programme, change the information stored or misuse the information he or she is entitled to receive.

Privacy safeguards cost money. The Government's White Paper stresses the need to keep expenditure to the minimum and ensure that the new Data Protection Authority is self-financing. Penny-pinching is going to result in inadequate privacy controls — especially in those existing computerised systems which did not have privacy safeguards built in to start with and are therefore expensive to modify. What the public needs to consider is the extent to which they want to control information about themselves. Some information — exam results; records of vaccinations — may be considered comparatively unimportant, needing only minimum safeguards to ensure that it is only available to those authorised to have it. But other information — medical records and details of mental ill-health — is so private, and so capable of abuse, that rigorous safeguards are essential, however expensive. Those who run the data banks may claim that they cannot afford to do so if they are required to improve their security procedures, to code the data to reduce the risk of unauthorised access, to allow the individual to see the record and correct it and to maintain a regular review of those who have had access to information in order to detect any fraud or abuse. The answer is simple: if a data bank cannot afford to guarantee the privacy which the community requires, then it should not operate at all.

---

1) out of print; library copies at NCCL
2) *Privacy and the Law,* Justice 1970
3) *Privacy, Computers and You,* NCCL and the National Computing Centre Ltd 1970
4) *Computers and Privacy,* Cmnd 6353 HMSO December 1975

5) *Computers: Safeguards for Privacy*, Cmnd 6354 HMSO December 1975

6) Cmnd 6354, Table 5

7) 'Computers and Privacy', Dr G Niblett, *Privacy, Computers and You*

8) *Privacy and the Protection of Personal Information in Europe,* Staff report to the Committee on Government operations, US Senate, March 1975, p 40

9) Cmnd 6354, para 10

10) *The Assault on Privacy,* Miller, University of Michigan 1971

11) See 'The Crime Machine', *Guardian* 11 March 1977

12) *New Scientist* 19 December 1974

13) Cmnd 6353, para 23

14) *New Scientist,* 4 November 1976

National government

The machinery of modern government demands ever-increasing amounts of personal information. Services which are essential to the community — collection of taxes and administration of benefits; provision of education, transport and health services; the administration of justice and legal aid — cannot operate without disclosure of personal information. Defending privacy does *not* mean denying government the information it legitimately needs: it means instead ensuring that the individual, not the government, controls the collection and use of information.

Growing computerisation has aroused public fears of a technological, 1984-style Big Brother — a national data bank, with files on everyone, churning out lists of deviants to government inspectors. Government departments, local authorities and the police already hold between them enough information to compile a comprehensive profile of every citizen of the United Kingdom. The Government has declared that it has no intention of constructing such a data bank, or bringing together information now held by separate agencies[1]. The linking of files now kept separately would involve a fundamental breach of trust between government and the community but, given the extent to which information is already shared between different bodies, it is impossible to be confident that future governments will resist the temptation. Legislation is needed to give statutory force to the Government's pledge, ensuring that any Government which in future wanted to try and link up different data banks would have to declare its intentions and seek Parliamentary authority. This section describes the main data banks already held by national government and the safeguards which are needed for the individual's privacy.

OFFICE OF POPULATION, CENSUSES AND SURVEYS

A full-scale Census must balance two considerations — the need of society to take rational decisions about its future based on accurate information, and the right of the individual to control personal information. Most citizens will accept the need for proper surveys, in the reasonable expectation that social benefits will follow from them. Most people will co-operate with surveys of this kind, and in a healthy society it is desirable that they should wish to do so. At the same time, governments must realise that as citizens are prepared to trust governments in this matter, so governments must trust citizens to give their information properly and willingly, without criminal sanctions being employed.[2]

Neither the 1971 Census, nor the White Paper on the 1976 Census (which was cancelled on public expenditure grounds) satisfactorily achieved this balance. A number of individuals, outraged or distressed by the detailed questioning in the 1971 Census, were prosecuted for their refusal to complete the form. The justification offered for criminal sanctions is that 100% returns are essential for proper planning. It is, of course, impossible to ensure completely accurate and full returns and the White Paper itself admits that some figures will be rounded up before statistical information is made publicly available. The first purpose of the Census is to count the population, and NCCL believes that a compulsory questionnaire, concerning only name, date of birth, sex and usual place of residence, is needed to achieve this aim. For the rest, the Census should consist of an anonymous questionnaire, completion of which would be voluntary, which would cover all the other questions which the OPCS decided it needed to ask. The very fact of anonymity would make people more willing to complete questions on a wider range of topics.

In 1971, William Whitelaw MP gave a public undertaking that 'information about individual people or families will under no circumstances be released to any authority outside the Census organisation itself' (Hansard; 20 April 1971). Despite this guarantee of confidentiality, the OPCS undertook on behalf of the DHSS a follow-up survey of ex-nurses, whose names and addresses were obtained from the individual Census returns — although no warning that this could happen was given on the Census form. It is not good enough to allow the OPCS to distort a clear assurance given about the use of the Census by acting as an agent for other Government departments who wish to do follow-up surveys.

More disturbing is the statement in the 1975 White Paper that information will be compiled for 'smaller areas' (than local authority areas), without defining such areas. If 1971 practice is followed, the smaller areas will be wards, parishes and enumeration districts which cover between 50 and 200 households. The White Paper admits that, if the information for some smaller areas was published accurately, it would be possible to identify individuals from it. To avoid this possibility, figures will be 'rounded or otherwise adjusted'. Census information is sold to commercial organisations, who can thus obtain information on small groups of people and, by comparing the information with, for instance, the electoral register, may even be able to make fairly accurate predictions about the characteristics of identified individuals.

But the possibility of identification is not the only objection to the sale of Census information in small blocks. Some credit reference agencies mark people down as 'bad risks' not because they have a known history of debts, but because they live at the wrong address. Gas and electricity boards, for instance, may demand a deposit from people living in low-income areas even though the particular individual concerned has an impeccable credit history. Even without identifying individuals from Census data, a company may decide to discriminate against everyone living in a particular area which is shown by the Census to have certain general characteristics. The two risks of identification and misuse led NCCL to campaign for a restriction on the tabulation of Census information to areas no smaller than County District,

Metropolitan Area District or London borough.

More people complained about enumerators than any other aspect of the 1971 Census. As that Census showed, an enumerator may discover information in the course of the Census which he or she would find useful at work, for instance, in the local authority rating department. Thus, the wrong choice of enumerators can lead directly to a breach of confidentiality. Not only should enumerators have to make a declaration of confidentiality, but certain groups of public officials (tax inspectors, customs and excise and immigration officials, some local government officers, policemen) together with sales representatives and other business people should not be eligible for employment as enumerators.

Other surveys

Although the Census is the most comprehensive, compulsory survey of the population, OPCS also carry out other surveys for use by government. The General Household Survey, for instance, is a voluntary survey of about 15,000 households each year. Survey forms are identified by address, not by individuals' names, and the interviewers begin the survey by taking details about the rateable value of the premises occupied from the local authority valuation lists. The Survey provides extremely detailed information about household composition, place of birth, housing standards, rent and mortgage payments, economic activity, job satisfaction and mobility; leisure activities; health and use of the health services. In addition, the Survey identifies every person seen by the interviewer according to the interviewer's own estimate of the person's colour.

In 1973, about 70% of those interviewed answered all the questions; 13% refused to co-operate at all; and 7% co-operated only in part. Not surprisingly, the questions about income are most likely to meet with a refusal of information.

General Household Survey returns are, of course, confidential. But because they provide sensitive personal details about people who could be identified with a high degree of accuracy, it is essential that forms be destroyed after the information is coded and computerised, or that the statistical information be kept separately from the list of addresses sampled. Such precautions (which we also propose for medical research information; on page 45) should be standard procedure in statistical surveys and should be backed by legislation which would also forbid any other Government department gaining access to information about individuals. It would also be helpful if instructions to interviewers, and the published Survey report, spelled out the precautions which are taken to ensure confidentiality.

DEPARTMENT OF HEALTH AND SOCIAL SECURITY

The DHSS keeps computerised records of individuals' National Insurance (Social Security) contributions. Entitlement to benefit depends on having an adequate contributions record, together with proof of the condition (retirement; maternity; sickness; unemployment) to which benefit is linked.

Contribution records will be used in future to decide how much pension an individual is entitled to under the new, earnings-related scheme which begins in April 1978. The formula for deciding the pension involves recording the average level of earnings during the 20 highest years' of earnings (taking into account the effect of inflation), making allowance for years spent at home with 'home responsibilities' and calculating a flat-rate and an earnings-related pension. Even if the DHSS provide each contributor with an annual record of contributions paid and earnings level, an individual wanting to challenge his or her pension entitlement in the twenty-first century may be faced with trying to correct an error made years previously and undetected at the time.

Local social security offices also maintain files giving the work history of unemployed workers, in order to establish entitlement to benefit. Someone dismissed for misconduct, for instance, may be refused unemployment benefit. In 1976, files held by the Wimbledon office were found in dustbins behind a block of flats.[3] The files gave the name, address, national insurance number, marital status and work record of about fifty people. For instance, the file of a GPO worker dismissed for unsatisfactory conduct listed how many times he had been late or absent from work and said that, after warnings, the GPO had sacked him. Another described a woman clerk who was 'eased out' of her job after asking for a pay rise; the woman left her job without working out her notice. Although a claimant who appeals against refusal of national insurance benefit will obtain some documentation on the reasons for refusal, there is no right of access to the full record.

Unemployed workers are also the subject of records held by local employment offices, which collect 'both basic factual information about each person registered and also notes and objective assessments made by employment office staff designed to assist them in seeking out suitable employment.' One unemployed man who claims to have seen his record told NCCL that the record included information about all previous employment and personal comments by the clerks which 'can be seriously astray'. This man also complained of errors in job descriptions and classifications in the record of previous employment. The department insists that 'the records are confidential and it is the policy of the Agency not to disclose them except upon order of the court.'[4]

Although employment offices need to hold records on people seeking work, such records should be seen by the person concerned who could correct any inaccuracies or challenge the opinions expressed. Some people, for whom it is difficult or impossible to find work, may be distressed by seeing their files. But this risk does not outweigh the advantages to be gained by honest disclosure of the record, and a right to challenge inaccurate or irrelevant information or remarks. Errors in a credit reference file — which is now open for inspection — usually lead only to a refusal of credit; errors in an employment file can lead to a loss of livelihood.

Supplementary benefits

Over 4½ million people are the subjects of extremely sensitive personal files held by the local offices which administer the supplementary benefits system. Because benefits depend on a test of someone's income, expenditure and family condition, officials administering the scheme need to collect detailed and often intimate information about the claimant's private life. Pensioners, in particular, often refuse to claim means-tested benefits precisely because they are scared of intrusion into their private lives by officials who may misuse the information they acquire.

Supplementary benefits claimants include pensioners, the unemployed or ill, and single parents, together with their families. The files kept on them do not appear in the Government's record of computerised data banks since they are, at present anyway, kept manually. This means that the proposed new Data Protection Authority will not have any control over them. But social security files may contain information which is inaccurate, malicious or irrelevant and may be used as the basis for denying an individual benefits which are not calculated on a statutory basis, but which depend on the official's discretion. The case quoted on page 1 shows how offensive such a file may be.

In 1976, a claimants' union in Leicester obtained a file going back 20 years on a woman claimant. According to those who saw the file, it included information about her sexual relationship with her husband, intimate medical details, personal letters from social workers and family photos she had sent to the Queen when pleading for help over her social security payments. Another claimant who caught sight of her file complained to the Northumberland and Durham NCCL that the folder contained local press cuttings about her.

Until August 1977, the Supplementary Benefits Commission banned certain groups from Government re-establishment centres. A civil servant, in a letter to MIND (National Association for Mental Health) said that it was normal to exclude 'men whose physical and mental disabilities make it very unlikely that they can be fitted for regular employment; homosexuals; men who have committed offences such as larceny and assault and habitual drunkards'. This practice indicates the kind of information collected by SBC officials on claimants and used to exclude certain people from potential benefits. After the rule was publicised in the *Guardian,* the chairperson of the SBC ordered that the rule should be rewritten.

The worst examples of invasion of privacy by supplementary benefits officers result from the operation of the 'cohabitation rule', which states that, where a man and woman are living together as 'husband and wife', their resources and needs must be combined and benefit claimed by the man. In 1954, the DHSS employed only 16 special investigators (one of whose main jobs is to investigate suspected cohabitation); in 1976 they employed 397 (although 26 posts were unfilled). Popularly known as 'sex snoopers', the investigators often rely on anonymous information or gossip to trigger off an enquiry. They may wait outside a woman's home in order to catch a boyfriend leaving early in the morning. They may question other people — the boyfriend; neighbours; the man's employer or workmates; the landlord or landlady; the woman's children (although they are instructed not to question children, Child Poverty Action Group has received complaints about investigators who have in fact done so.) Widows on national insurance benefit may also be investigated, since their widow's pension is withdrawn on remarriage or cohabitation.

Special investigators are guided by instructions in the A and AX Codes — which the Supplementary Benefits Commission has consistently refused to publish. A CPAG study[5] of the operation of the cohabitation rule, based in part on a study of the secret codes, showed that — despite the Commission's public emphasis on an impartial consideration of the facts, and the need to avoid unnecessary invasions of privacy — the secret codes placed great stress on the need to catch the claimant out. For instance, the AX code stressed that the aim of the observation was, not to establish whether or not cohabitation might exist, but 'to provide evidence of the man's movements that lead to the conclusion that he lives in the claimant's accommodation'. Although investigators have no right of entry to private homes without the occupier's consent, a number of women complained to CPAG that the investigator had insisted on being shown round the house and allowed to inspect people's clothes and bedrooms. The Commission published a new report on the cohabitation rule in March 1976, but has not published any changes to the secret codes. If the cohabitation rule is to remain, the secret codes must be published so that the public can judge whether the instructions given to investigators are likely to lead to proper respect for claimants' privacy.

Another CPAG study[6] showed how single mothers are particularly likely to face intrusive questioning by supplementary benefits officials.

> An unmarried mother was visited by an officer from a Liverpool office who questioned her persistently about the identity of her baby's father. The woman wanted to protect the father, who is married with children, and finally replied that she did not know who the father was. The visiting officer asked 'for the names of all possible fathers', saying that 'we (the local office) will sort out who the father is.'
>
> A divorced wife with four children was also put under unusual pressure to name the father of her young twins (who are not her husband's children). When she was in hospital, she had continued to receive benefit, not knowing that it should be reduced. She was subsequently threatened with 'six months inside' unless she named the father. As he is married and she no longer saw him, she had resolutely refused to name him. But under this new pressure she had to humiliate herself and said untruthfully that she had met him at a party and did not know his name. Every time she is visited, she has to sign a

statement to say that she has not seen him.

The officials who administer the supplementary benefits scheme are often poorly paid and over-worked. As the CPAG report points out, it is not surprising if some of them resent the additional demands which single mothers may create because of the stress they are under or if they share the widespread mythology about 'welfare scroungers'. The confidential code of instructions for officers dealing with single mothers stresses 'the avoidance of unnecessary expenditure of public funds' and the need to ensure that the father of the children pays for their upkeep, even though, in a large number of cases, the father could not afford to do so. A single mother receiving supplementary benefits does *not* have to name the father of the child, but, given the emphasis on finding the father, it is perhaps not surprising that officials so often do not inform the woman of her rights.

In the words of the CPAG report: 'Single mothers are among the most vulnerable people in our society . . . . For the majority living on supplementary benefit, life is a bleak struggle to keep themselves on the official poverty line.' Thus, people with the least power and the least resources in the community are also least able to protect their privacy by controlling information about their personal lives.

Children

Since the White Paper on government computers was published in December 1975, the DHSS has announced the birth of a new data bank — the National Standard Register and Recall System for Child Health Purposes.[7]) This impressively-titled system, which received almost no publicity at its launch, will cover every child born in Britain. Information will be gathered from the health visitor when she visits the mother soon after the birth, and from schools health programmes. The computer will initially be used for the immunisation programme and later for other health programmes in schools. The DHSS will therefore possess confidential information about everyone born in this country after 1976.

INLAND REVENUE AND VAT

Public concern over privacy has focussed in the last few years on the increased powers given to tax and VAT inspectors, and on alleged abuses of those powers.

The Finance Act 1972 gave VAT officers a power to enter people's homes or workplaces without a warrant, although, in order to carry out a search, they had to obtain a magistrate's warrant. Where a self-employed trader or a partner in a small firm works from home or from offices attached to the home, VAT officials may find it necessary to enter and, in some cases, search private accommodation. Most of the complaints have arisen in these circumstances. Early in 1975, a dozen dealers in Yorkshire complained about the conduct of VAT officials. One owner of an antique shop said that the officials stayed for about four hours, seized 'every scrap of paper I had with names and figures written on, took away my personal address and telephone book, searched my toilet, my car, my handbag and read my personal diary.' Another alleged that his house, warehouse and 18-year-old daughter's bedroom were searched.

According to the report of the Commissioners for Customs and Excise for 1974/75, all these complaints were thoroughly investigated. The report states that: 'About 240,000 control visits of this kind were made during the year and, in a good many cases, this was the trader's first personal contact with a VAT officer. The need for a reasonably thorough verification had been generally appreciated, and encouragingly little complaint about these visits has been made. However, shortly before the end of the year under review, considerably publicity was given to allegations that VAT officers had exceeded or abused their powers or had behaved in an unreasonable manner. These allegations related to ten visits in all, though the repetition of the complaints gave the impression of a much larger number. Immediate and thorough investigation, moreover, disclosed no justification for the allegations, except in two relatively minor instances. (On one occasion an officer had examined the contents of a wastepaper basket without permission, and on another an officer had opened the drawers of a desk without permission.)'

In April 1975, the Minister of State at the Home Office, Alex Lyon MP, announced that two VAT officials had been disciplined as a result of investigations following these complaints of misconduct.

NCCL has also received complaints from traders concerned at the extent of VAT officials' powers. According to one shopkeeper, three VAT officials entered his shop and, while one explained the purpose of the visit, the other two began rummaging, without his permission, in his papers at the back of the shop. He asked them to wait until he had given them permission and to make the search in his presence, and they left, threatening to return with a search warrant.

It is clear that only a tiny proportion of VAT inspectors' visits result in complaints. But the dangers of abuse by individuals is evident, given the combination of complex legislation demanding detailed financial information from the individuals affected, and the power for officials to enter without a warrant or obtain a search warrant.

The Finance Act 1976 gives similar, although more restricted powers, to tax inspectors, by giving them the right to enter and search private premises and remove documents, on a warrant from a Circuit judge. They have also been given the power to question a suspect's spouse and children. Unlike the powers of VAT officials, which can be used in the everyday course of business, the tax inspectors' powers relate only to cases of suspected fraud and, according to the Chancellor, will be used only in a handful of cases where serious fraud is suspected and other methods, such as a requisition for the documents by the Inland Revenue Commissioners, have failed. The proposal caused considerable outcry amongst MPs and the press. NCCL proposed three amendments to provide safeguards against the possibility of abuse: firstly, that the power should be limited to cases of suspected fraud above a certain sum; secondly, that the warrant should only be obtainable from a High Court judge (and not, as originally proposed, a magistrate); and thirdly, that the suspect should be notified when the warrant had been obtained so that he and an adviser could be present to witness the search. In addition to restricting the power to grant warrants to circuit judges, the Chancellor amended the proposal so that an inspector could only apply for a warrant with the approval of a Commissioner for the Inland Revenue. Similar restrictions are needed on the wider powers of VAT officials.

The Inland Revenue already has wide powers to obtain information. Most information is provided by the individual, in tax returns and other communications. Banks are under an obligation to forward information to the Inland Revenue if it appears to concern liability for capital transfer tax, as are certain advisers (excluding accountants and lawyers). The Commissioners for Inland Revenue can issue a notice demanding production of certain documents; the penalty for withholding or falsifying information is £50 and £10 for each day until the documents are disclosed.

The report of the Royal Commission on Corruption in Public Life proposed that, on a warrant obtained by the Director of Public Prosecutions from a High Court Judge, the police should be able to get information from the Inland Revenue, if there are reasonable grounds to suspect that a public servant is involved in corruption. A minority report proposes that the Revenue themselves should take the initiative in passing on information to the DPP where they have 'a sufficiently strong suspicion of corruption to call for an investigation'. Lord Houghton, a member of the Commission, rightly criticised the minority proposal: 'I believe the firmest stand should now be taken on this simple principle; that information supplied by the citizen under the compulsion of the law to a government agency should not be used or passed on for purposes beyond that agency's statutory functions without the express authority of Parliament explicitly laying down the condition in which this may be permissible or even obligatory and the strict safeguards to be provided for the citizen against the abuse or arbitrary use of such far-reaching powers.'[8])

VEHICLE REGISTRATION AND DRIVER LICENCING

One source of information for the Inland Revenue is the Vehicle Registration and Licensing index at Swansea, which keeps information on all vehicle owners and car drivers with provisional or full licences. Up to date addresses of car drivers are given to the Inland Revenue to help them pursue tax evaders — although car-owners or drivers are not told by Swansea that information supplied for one purpose — in order to drive a car — is to be used for an entirely different purpose.

The Swansea Index also supplies information to the Police National Computer for its national index of vehicle owners, and to the Home Office who follow up parking tickets. Other Departments and local authorities who supply a reason for needing the information will also be given it on request.

In addition to vehicle details and the name and address of the car-owner or driver, the Index has information about the sex, date of birth, eyesight, medical history and motoring convictions of each licence-holder.

Most of the information held on the Index is, of course, supplied by the individual applying for a licence. The Department of the Environment which maintains the Index may also pursue anonymous tips, as the following case illustrates.

> Mrs O received a letter from an official in the drivers' medical enforcement section, ordering her to produce a certificate showing that her eyesight was up to standard, and stating that: 'A letter has been received at the licensing centre which throws doubt on your ability to meet the eyesight requirements necessary for the granting of a driving licence.' Mrs O's doctor tested her and found that she was quite fit to drive, but was so disturbed by the incident that he referred her to a solicitor. The Licensing Centre explained that they would not disclose the source of their information, but said they had been told that Mrs O had been involved in two accidents and that she would be prosecuted unless a certificate of eyesight was produced. Mrs O has never been prosecuted for a driving offence; she had not been involved in any collision; and no claim had been made on her and her husband's joint insurance policy.

There are adquate powers for the police and courts to have someone's eyesight checked without officials trying to do the job for them.

TELEVISION LICENSING

About 1 million people in this country neither own nor rent a television set. Few invasions of privacy seem to upset some of them more than the offensive letters dispatched from the National TV licence Records Office in Bristol, demanding — although without giving any statutory authority — immediate payment or explanation. The Wireless and Telegraph Act 1949 gives the Records Office the power to ask for information about licences, and to enter premises with a search warrant if necessary. A later Act gives the Postmaster General power to get information about people buying or renting TV sets from dealers. But the Records Office now uses a computerised index of all addresses in the country (apparently compiled by the Post Office for the purpose of allocating post codes) to send out a letter to every houshold without a TV licence, followed by a second letter and in some cases an inspector if no reply is received. Even where the householder replies that they do not have a TV, there is (according to a *New Scientist* report in 1974) a 1 in 4 chance that the computer will select the household, on a random basis, for an inspector's visit anyway.[9)]

It is, of course, a criminal offence to use a TV set without a licence. The BBC lose over £6 million each year in unpaid licence fees. So the computerised Records Office provides an opportunity to increase BBC revenue substantially. But the householder who does not use a TV — and who has an unqualified legal right to refuse to answer the inspector's questions or reply to the Office's letters — may strongly object to the harassment and threats of prosecution dealt out by the Office. The initial enquiry letters sent out at least refer to the possibility that the household does not have a TV set; the follow-up letter (after an unsuccessful visit by an inspector) does not even mention this possibility, except in the reply section, although there are more non-users than there are un-licensed users.

Even the licensed TV viewer may suffer, as the following letter to NCCL showed.

> 'My wife answered a knock on the front door. On opening the door there was a man standing there who said that he was from the Post Office and wanted to find out if we had a tv set in the house. Brushing past my wife (I was away at work at the time) this man marched into the living room where our tv set stands. The man then began to badger my wife with questions about whether she had a tv licence. My wife replied that she knew nothing about the tv licence (which was true because I always go to the local post office to renew our tv licence which is in my name as head of the family) . . . . (Two months later) the policeman delivered a recorded delivery letter to us which came from the Post Office. This letter contained a summons for my wife to appear at Croydon Petty Sessional Court on the charge of not having a tv licence . . . . I enclose a copy of our tv licence in my name.'

PUBLIC OFFICIALS WITH POWERS OF ENTRY

The powers of the police to enter people's homes, search and take items, have been considerably extended in the last decade by Acts of Parliament and by court decisions. The power to enter private premises also belongs to thousands of public officials, under at least 188 different statutory powers (in England and Wales; 81 in Scotland and 110 in Northern Ireland). Officials empowered, in certain circumstances, to enter private premises include wages inspectors; Health and Safety inspectors; DHSS officials (for instance, inspecting nursing homes, children's and foster homes); housing officials (to survey property for compulsory purchase orders, investigate sanitary conditions etc); fire inspectors; Gaming Board inspectors; Post Office officials; Atomic Energy Authority officials; Customs and Excise officers; and the officials of gas and electricity boards.[10]

In most cases, the power of entry is needed by officials doing a useful, necessary job — investigating safety provisions in a factory, for instance, or making sure that a nursing home comes up to the prescribed standards. But it is high time that the multitude of entry provisions was reviewed and a full list published. Neither the Treasury nor the Department of the Environment could provide a full answer to Parliamentary Questions on powers of entry for which they had responsibility. Except in cases of emergency, entry to someone's home should only be with a warrant, and there should be a code of conduct ensuring that, with only a few exceptions, advance notice and an explanation of the reasons for the entry are given to the occupier. The 24 hours' notice given, for instance, for visits in connection with local authority planning or compulsory purchase orders, is inadequate, particularly when postal delays mean that the written notice arrives after the official.

It is important to stress that officials' powers of entry are not systematically abused, and there are few complaints. But courtesy and common-sense on the part of today's officials is no excuse for Government and Parliament to go on adding to public powers of entry, without firstly ensuring that each power is strictly necessary and that safeguards are instituted to minimise the risk of future abuse.

---

(1) Cmnd 6354, para 10

(2) See NCCL Memorandum on the 1976 Census, March 1975

(3) *Guardian,* 13 August 1976

(4) Letter from Parliament Under Secretary of State, Department of Employment, July 1975

(5) *As Man and Wife?,* Ruth Lister, Poverty research series 2, Child Poverty Action Group (undated)

(6) *Social Insecurity,* Jane Streather and Stuart Weir, Poverty pamphlet 16, Child Poverty Action Group 1974

(7) *New Scientist,* 20 May 1976

(8) *Times,* 19 July 1976

(9) *New Scientist,* 14 November 1974

(10) Hansard: Written answers to questions tabled by David Price MP (21 July 1976)

Local government

Much of the complex social and financial provision required by the community is administered by local authorities, not by Whitehall. Local government is, therefore, responsible for collecting and maintaining detailed information on individuals and families in their area. Local education authorities and schools keep detailed records on both teachers and pupils; the housing department holds files on tenants and rate-payers; social work departments keep records, often containing extremely sensitive information, on their clients, including families where injury to a child is suspected, and the mentally ill. As a major employer, local government keeps personnel records on its own workers. As the administrators of nearly forty means-tested financial benefits (including rent and rate rebates and educational welfare grants), local authorities collect detailed information on the income and expenditure of millions of families. And for planning purposes, local authorities carry out their own statistical surveys, usually identifiable at least by address, if not by name.

Each local authority department, therefore, possesses a considerable quantity of personal information on part of the community; together, they cover, in varying degrees of detail, nearly every individual and family in the area. Although social workers in particular have developed a code of ethics to protect the client's confidentiality (discussed in detail below), there are no legal restraints on the information which a local authority department may collect, or the use to which it is put.

In November 1975, the *Daily Mirror* reported that Spelthorne Council in Staines, Middlesex, maintained files on ratepayers and tenants which included newspaper cuttings of even minor motoring offences. The leader of the Council was reported as defending the practice on the grounds that the Council needed information in order to prove to a court that a rates or rent defaulter could in fact pay the bills. Quite apart from the haphazard nature of collecting details on reported motoring offences only, there are proper legal procedures for obtaining such information from someone taken to court for not paying a debt.

In 1976, NCCL received a copy of the following letter sent by Multibroadcast Colour TV Rentals to the Director of Housing in Hounslow, Middlesex:

> 'I refer to the telephone conversation between a member of your staff and my Area Arrears Controller, concerning the above mentioned who resided at the above address.
> 'I have been given to understand that he has now been rehoused by you, and upon written application from this office you would be prepared to forward to me his present address so that we may

> ascertain the whereabouts of our equipment. This information will of course be treated in the strictest confidence, and from where it was obtained will not be divulged.'

It is, of course, entirely contrary to the principle that information should only be used for the purpose for which it is obtained, for a local authority to provide information about a council tenant either to a commercial company or to a public authority such as the gas or electricity board. As we propose later, it should in fact be unlawful to do so.

Some local authorities, in an attempt to reduce rent arrears, have taken to alerting the press when people are taken to court for arrears. Although councils believe that the publicity will 'shame' tenants into paying their debts, some social and community workers have expressed concern about the effect on their own relationship with the families, and the unfairness of penalising families further in a time of rapid inflation. In one local newspaper report[1], 17 families were named, along with the details of their income, whether employed or not, the number of children and amount of family allowance received, the arrears due, and their address. Virtually all of the families were either earning below-average wages, or receiving social security. Although court hearings are, of course, public, it is rare for such cases to be reported in detail.

People asked to complete detailed questionnaires for statistical surveys may also worry about the confidentiality of their answers.

> Mr and Mrs W complained about the conduct of a field worker employed by Wandsworth Borough Council while carrying out a survey. The aim of the survey was to establish the number of households in the area, and the number of people in each household. The Council stated that it was sometimes necessary to approach next-door neighbours if people were out at each visit by the survey worker. The W's returned home one evening to find that the survey worker had been questioning their neighbours in some detail, suggesting that the W's lived in a 'commune'. They received an apolgy from the Council, and were also assured that the survey forms were securely kept and would be destroyed as soon as the survey was complete.

Social work records

Social workers are well aware of the confidential nature of information given them by clients. The British Association of Social Workers, in its report on confidentiality in social work, has this to say: 'Within this relationship the client may disclose information about himself and his family of a highly personal and emotionally charged nature. He shares such information as part of the process of receiving help and it is in this context he realises the necessity for disclosure. . . . Sometimes his needs cannot be met by the social worker alone but will require the skills of other professions; he may need help to accept this and the necessity for pertinent information to be transferred on the understanding that the social worker will not divulge confidential information entrusted to him for one purpose for use in another without his sanction.'[2])

BASW also proposes five situations in which the social worker may decide to override the client's right of confidentiality:
- when the client's own life is in danger;
- where there is serious danger to other people;
- where there is a serious threat of violence to the social worker;
- where there is serious threat to the community;
- in other 'exceptional circumstances' as decided on the basis of 'professional consideration and consultation'.

A number of cases, some of which are quoted in the BASW report, illustrate that confidentiality is not always properly observed.

> At a supplementary benefits tribunal hearing, a letter from a social worker about a client was read out by the Department of Health and Social Security officer as evidence that the claimant should not receive a special needs grant. The claimant had to sit in front of the tribunal and listen to a ruthless recital of his alleged weaknesses, ending up with the statement that the social worker had 'washed his hands of the family'.[3])
>
> NCCL was approached recently by Mr D who lives in a voluntary organisation hostel for single men. At a group meeting in the hostel, the hostel worker had read out the social worker's report on Mr D, which said that Mr D had been convicted of trying to murder his GP and given a suspended sentence. Mr D says that his conviction was for something quite different, a minor homosexual offence, and claims that his doctor supports him. NCCL is taking the case up with the local authority involved and the hostel worker.

In neither of these cases had the client been asked to consent to the communication of a report to other people; nor had they been shown the contents of the report first.

BASW points out that it is inevitable, within a social services department, that each social worker will share information with other social workers, as well as with administrative workers, such as the perison who types up a report. BASW quotes the case of an adoptive mother, congratulated on her success in adopting a baby by her neighbour, who happened to be the local authority typist who typed up the adoption report. Not surprisingly, the mother made a strong complaint about breach of confidence.

In 1975, a social work lecturer carried out an experiment to test the confidentiality of social work records. Ten researchers, mainly social work students, obtained written consent from people who were clients of various social work agencies. The researchers then posed as social workers and phoned the organisations, asking for confidential information about the clients. Out of sixteen agencies contacted, only once was information refused.[4])

Social workers are increasingly likely to share information with people outside their own department. In a case involving a family with children, for instance, the social worker may need to work with the family doctor, the hospital authorities, the school which the children attend, the educational psychologist, the NSPCC, the police, probation officer and the juvenile court. Social workers also prepare reports on defendants in criminal cases, where the judge or magistrate asks for a social enquiry report. In adoption proceedings, a social worker may be appointed as *guardian ad litem* in order to prepare a report on the fitness of the prospective adoptors. Similarly, social workers may be asked to prepare reports in divorce proceedings involving a dispute over custody of the children, or in wardship cases.

In court proceedings, the person who is the subject of a social work report may be entitled to see the report — but not always. In adult criminal courts, a copy of any social enquiry report must be given to the defendant or his or her lawyer. If the defendant is a juvenile (under 17) and comes up in an adult court (i.e., where the young person is charged with adults, or charged with homicide), the report must be given to the lawyer, or the parent or guardian if they are in court, but not to the young person himself. Social enquiry reports are not usually read out in court.

In the juvenile court, the parents or guardian must be told about anything in the report which the magistrates have taken account of, although, in practice, many courts show a copy of the full report to the parents. In adoption proceedings, the report of the *guardian ad litem* is confidential, although it must be shown to a prospective adoptor if it makes allegations about his or her fitness to adopt. In wardship cases, the parties have no absolute right to see reports on the child, but the judge must decide whether to withhold a report.

It used to be the case in magistrates' courts hearing domestic cases, that welfare reports were read aloud. Now they must be shown to the parties or their lawyers but must also be read out if the court decides.

The BASW report, which sets out these different provisions[5], comments that 'Natural justice might be thought to demand that a person should know exactly what is said about him to a tribunal which will judge him'. Indeed, it does, and the law should be amended accordingly.

Given the network of people who may see a social work report, or discuss information about a case it is particularly important — but also particularly difficult — to ensure confidentiality. Rigorous rules about the security of storage and the use (preferably, non-use) of telephones are vital, as are measures to ensure that secretaries and other workers within the social work agency are fully aware of the need for confidentiality. Social workers also need to consider the implications of handing over reports or information to workers who are not bound by the same professional code, and detailed guidelines are needed, possibly with statutory backing, setting out the agencies to whom it is proper to give information. It is quite improper, for instance, for a social security presenting officer to be able to obtain a social worker's report on a claimant for supplementary benefits.

Amongst all the individuals and agencies who may see a social work report, the one person who will not see it is the individual who is the subject of the report. The BASW report on confidentiality states that, although the social worker may decide that it would help the client to see his or her file, the file itself is the property of the agency and will normally not be shown to the individual concerned. Although the Association clearly attaches great value to confidentiality, and emphasises the need for trust between the social worker and the client, its report gives no reasons to justify this general rule of secrecy.

The first argument which may be offered to justify withholding the record from the individual is that the file does not 'belong' to the client — it is the property of the agency which compiles it. On the other hand, BASW quotes approvingly an American professional association's view that 'the record stands instead of the person and should be treated with the same consideration due the consumer as a person'. If property rights are to be used as a basis for defining the right to privacy (which is dubious) it is surely more helpful to recognise that a social work file does 'belong' to the person on whom that file is held — the client has given the social worker much of the information on the file, and provided the means of obtaining more. Secondly, it may be said that a social worker could not comment as freely if the file were to be seen by the client. That may well be true, and the restraint would be thoroughly desirable if it stopped social workers from making comments which they could not justify. It is also, however, important to distinguish between notes which a social worker may make for his or her own use, which do not form part of a permanent record and are not (or should not be) communicated to others, and comments or conclusions which become part of a permanent record, available to other workers. If the social worker's opinions are to become part of a communicated record, then they should be communicated to the individual, as well as to others. Thirdly, a social work report may well contain information obtained in confidence about others, for instance, in the same family. Such a situation may justify partial withholding of the file from the individual concerned: but withholding of information should be justified as an exception to a general rule.

More positively, it is fundamentally unfair for crucial decisions to be taken about someone's life on the basis of a record or report which that person has never seen and whose contents he or she cannot challenge. There may be inaccuracies on the report, which will most quickly be revealed by personal inspection. There may be comments based on a misunderstanding of the situation, or where the client feels that a fuller explanation needs to be given. There may be material which is irrelevant and should be deleted. It may be more difficult for the social worker who will have to justify a record to the client; but opening the record to the client could also contribute to a more honest and trusting relationship. A general right of access for the client may, in exceptional cases, need to be withheld. In these circumstances, the worker should attach a written note to the file, explaining the grounds on which access has been denied.

Register of 'children at risk'

The conflict between individual privacy and protecting others is particularly acute with registers of children who may be at risk of injury. The death of Maria Colwell and other children at the hands of a member of their own family led to strong public demands for better coordination between different social agencies. Local authoriy social services departments are increasingly likely to maintain a register of families where the children are thought to be at risk, using information gained from social workers themselves, doctors, teachers, hospitals, the NSPCC and others.

Like any other collection of information, 'at risk' registers suffer from the risk of inaccuracy. Because of the pressure on social workers to spot every potential tragedy, and the impossiblity of accurate predictions, a family may be placed on the register who have never harmed their child. It is NSPCC policy not to inform the family why they have been placed on the register. One family, having discovered they were suspected of battering their child, has sued the NSPCC for libel, claiming that the child has 'soft bones'. That case had not been finally heard at the time of writing. The following case, reported in the *Guardian,* illustrates the possible injustice of a register.

> Mrs A discovered that her 16-month old daughter was on the register kept by the social services department in Oxfordshire. She asked the department to remove the child's name since she had never been battered, and was in no danger of being battered by either her or her husband. A social worker refused to delete the child's name and, according to Mrs A, said that if the child fell or had a bruise when a social worker calls, the thought of non-accidental injury would lead the social worker to take the child away. Mrs A suffered a nervous breakdown at college, has been treated by a psychiatrist and, at one stage during the pregnancy, contemplated an abortion. But, she says, it is appallingly unfair to assume from this that she is likely to batter a 'much loved' daughter. The other piece of evidence which led to the child's inclusion on the register was that, when asking for a childminder for one day a week, Mrs A apparently said, 'who will stop me battering my baby' if she did not get a minder. Mrs A does not remember the conversation, but says that this remark should not be sufficient to put her name irrevocably on a register. (*Guardian* 3 May 1976).

In the hope of preventing injury to children, a decision may be taken to place on the register families which show a certain combination of characteristics — for instance, a mother who has had a nervous breakdown, considered an abortion during the pregnancy and referred to the possibility of battering the child — on the basis that there is a higher probability of battering in such families. The result may be to prevent tragedy in some families; but other families who never injure their children will inevitably find themselves on the register as well.

The local authorities' powers to take children into care were strengthened in 1975 by the Children Act, which allows a local authority to pass a resolution taking over parental rights and duties in respect of a child where it believes that the natural parents are incapable or unfit to act as parents. The parents must be given notice in writing after the resolution is passed, and have one month to object, after which the resolution either lapses or the local authority applies to the juvenile court for a hearing. In a case reported by the press in August 1977, a mother found herself forbidden to take her new-born baby home with her; when she returned two days later to collect the child, she was met by police and social workers who informed her that the local authority had taken the child into its care. The decision to seek a care order had apparently been taken at a case conference called some time previously, at which the couple's solicitor was present, but the couple (whose three older children were also in local authority care) had not been informed. (They had sacked their solicitor by the time the case was reported.) While the decision to take the baby into care may well have been the right one, it is disturbing that such a decision could have been taken, with the knowledge of the solicitor, but without any warning being given to the parents, even at the time when the mother came to leave hospital. With such extensive powers available to local authorities, the accuracy of 'at risk' registers becomes an issue of vital importance.

Refusal to be honest with the parents about the reasons for suspecting them of harming their child may lead the parents to distrust or refuse to see anyone connected with officialdom, as the case of Mr M quoted in the introduction (page 2) illustrates. Parents may well resent having their 'guilt' registered, with the prospect of losing their child and having to fight for custody in a court — even though no-one has told them why they are suspected. Parents who feel themselves least able to cope with officials, and who fear having a child taken into care, perhaps as a result of poverty, bad housing or mental illness, may begin to withdraw from the medical services or refuse to see social workers if they feel they are being labelled as 'batterers' unfairly. A register is a useful tool in the attempt to protect children from harm. But its existence must be publicly declared. The criteria used to decide who should be added to the list should be debated by local councillors on the social services committee and openly published. Parents should be told if their child has been added to the register, and should be able to appeal against their inclusion, preferably to an independent, informal tribunal. Not only is such a procedure fair to suspected parents, but honest discussion of the social worker's suspicions, backed by offers of help, could make a real contribution to reducing the risk of harm to the children. In law, a register of children at risk should be covered by 'qualified privilege', so that a parent whose name was placed on the list fairly, or as a result of a genuine mistake, would not be able to get damages for libel. But a parent whose name is added maliciously or negligently should have a legal redress.

Computerisation

Local authorities increasingly use computers to store their information.

In 1971, 339 local government computers were in use. By April 1975, this had grown to 573. Local authority computerised data banks include information about rents and rates; personnel records on employees; electoral registers — which may be bought by commercial bodies and given free to local political parties — and education and social service records.

The computer may also be used, as in the London Borough of Hammersmith, to streamline means-tested financial benefits. A single form is used to cover all benefits and the computer provides information about whether or not the applicant is claiming or receiving other benefits for which he or she is eligible. This can make life considerably easier for the claimant, who otherwise has to fill in a multitide of forms for different benefits — assuming that the claimant is even aware of the different benefits available. But it may also cause fears that the very detailed information provided on, for instance, an application form for a rent rebate will then be made available to other departments. Where such a system is used, it is important that, firstly, the form used should explain the procedure to the claimant and provide the claimant with an opportunity to stop his or her name being passed to other departments as being eligible for further benefits; and, secondly, that the detailed information should not be made available to other local authority workers.

The Local Authorities Management Service and Computer Committee (LAMSAC) has produced a comprehensive survey of local authorities' computing requirements based on contacts with fifty local authorities and allied bodies.[6] Their report uses three 'data bases' — people, property and resources — to establish a picture of the amount of information which might be stored.

The personal data base contains the following suggested information heads: geocode (i.e. address), date of birth and a link number so that different records about the same person can be matched up; marital status, relationships and legal status within the family; electoral status, credit rating, car ownership, socio-economic status (for planning, and to give background information on school pupils); nationality, place of birth, date of entry into the United Kingdom and languages; school records, including aptitude tests and exam results; academic record after leaving school; recreational activities; jobs held by school pupils and careers advice given; adults' occupation, hours of work and income; medical and mental health history and handicaps; social welfare records; juvenile offences; housing records; referrals from one department to another; and local authority manpower records, including performance appraisal.

The LAMSAC study, although not a blueprint on how data should actually be organised by computer, demonstrates the possibility of linking up information now held in separate departments. It stresses that security features must be provided to prevent unauthorised use of the information, and that each contributor and user of the information should agree on the legitimate uses to which 'their' data can be put.

LAMSAC envisages an increasing use of remote terminals, allowing officials in different offices to feed information into the system and to obtain, within a few seconds, whatever information they require and are permitted to have. The report says that, although many of the present local authority computers are unsuitable for remote terminals, 'encouragingly, a high proportion of the new computer orders are for machine types which are eminently suitable to teleprocessing.' Remote terminals make it dramatically easier for a large number of people to obtain detailed information about every individual within the local authority area covered by the computer system. Although it is possible to 'code' the system so that, for instance, only the social workers responsible for a particular family can see the printout of a family's record, it is hard to believe that other officials — for instance, housing officials making a decision about housing allocation — will, if the decision is left to them, resist the temptation to have comprehensive information about that family. The point is that the decision must not be left to them.

The quantity of information maintained by local authorities, the sensitivity of much of it, and the effects of increasing computerisation, make adequate safeguards for the individual a matter of urgency. Legislation is needed, administered by a Data Protection Authority, to make unauthorised access a criminal offence and to provide a right for the individual to see and correct the record. Professional codes for different groups of workers, together with the disciplinary provisions for local authority employees, should place great emphasis on ensuring confidentiality. Local authority workers themselves are subjects of files which are mostly kept secret from them: they therefore have as much interest in protecting individual privacy as the rest of the population.

A local authority's files may be of considerable interest to a government department such as the Inland Revenue; private commercial agencies or credit reference firms; private detectives, nosy neighbours or potential blackmailers. The first safeguard needed is control on access to the authority's information bank by people outside the authority. Strict criteria should define the circumstances which demand a transfer of information, for instance from social workers to the police, and as a general rule the individual's consent should be expressly sought first. The Law Commission has suggested[7] that it should be a criminal offence to deceive someone into giving information which otherwise would not have been given or, at least, to deceive someone into giving information which he or she was under a duty not to disclose to an unauthorised person. Either offence could be drafted to cover obtaining unauthorised information from a computer, for instance where someone not authorised to have the information had succeeded in obtaining the relevant code. Similarly, it should be an offence willingly to provide confidential information to someone not authorised to possess it. Such an extension of the criminal law is essential to protect the extremely sensitive information maintained by local authorities and other agencies.

But unauthorised users may be found *within* the local authority as well as outside it. There is, for instance, a danger that information given to one department for a specific purpose will be used as the basis for an adverse decision on an individual or family by an entirely different department. A social case-work record, perhaps commenting on a family's inadequacy, together with information about a history of mental illness, might influence a decision by the housing department — if the housing department had access to those files. The principle that information given or collected for one purpose should only be used for that purpose, and that the individual must consent to any new use, must be applied to the internal use of local authority information banks.

In a computerised system, each category of information can be coded according to its degree of sensitivity, and the appropriate code allocated to those officials with the right to see the information or add to it. Some information is publicly available — for instance, electoral registers, phone directories, county court judgment lists. That does not, however, mean that it should be freely available to local government officials. Information from the electoral register or phone book needs no special protection, although the sale of copies of the electoral register (as distinct from having it open for inspection) is open to challenge as a breach of the principle that information obtained for one purpose should not be used for another without consent. But information from a county court list can only now be obtained by request and on payment of a fee, and should not be made available to every potential user of a computerised system. At one end of any scale of confidentiality is public information which is already easily accessible and which can be given a low code in a computerised system. At the other end, is highly confidential information given only to one or a few trusted people — medical information, particularly concerning mental illness, sexually-transmitted diseases and gynaecological problems; social work and other records on family situations, especially involving illegitimacy, adoption or incest. Such information, if it is to be computerised at all, must be stored in such a way that only the physician or social worker who entered the information can have access to it, and any new would-be user would have to obtain authorisation from the individual concerned. But since it is impossible to provide an absolute guarantee of security for a computerised system, it is probably better to acknowledge that there is some information which is so sensitive that it should never be computerised at all. Any record of such information should be the personal responsibility of the doctor or social worker involved.

Limits should also be set on the period for which particular kinds of information may be stored. The Rehabilitation of Offenders Act 1974 provides for some convictions to become 'spent' after a set period, although this protection does not apply, for instance, where someone is involved in proceedings relating to adoption, guardianship, custody of a child or a care order. While the social services department will on occasion need information about spent convictions, any record of a conviction must be given a particularly restricted coding after it becomes spent. Aptitude tests at school are only useful while the pupil is at school; academic records, except examination results, should not be retained for more than a few years after the student has left the school or college. Information concerning a child, for instance where battering is suspected, should be deleted after a specified time-limit, and so on. One of the tasks of the new Data Protection Authority should be to draw up detailed guidelines for such time-limits.

Safeguards for a computerised system must also take into account the danger that, by recording a value judgment, the computer programme may give it the status of fact. A file containing a social worker's judgment that she has 'washed her hands of the Jones's' may not do much harm (unless, of course, it is read out at a supplementary benefits tribunal). But an 'X' code against the family's name is potentially the basis for refusing that family a series of local authority services. The social worker's judgment may reflect more on him or her than on the family; but it is the family which suffers. Personal opinions and judgements should not be entered on any computerised information system.

Some of the information which the LAMSAC study envisaged in its 'people' data base was in fact only needed for planning purposes — for instance, information about people's spare time interests was to be used to plan recreation provision. Where statistical information only is needed, the name or address of the individuals from whom the information has been obtained should not be recorded, or should be kept in an index, separate from the detailed information (as proposed on page 45 for other statistical and research records).

Finally, the development of local government records makes it even more important to give individuals, including local government workers, a legal right to see the information held on them, to challenge its accuracy and, if necessary, to insert a correction or alternative view. Where there are circumstances which justify denying access, these should be narrowly-defined exceptions to the general rule in favour of access. The right of access is now enforced for credit reference agencies. These safeguards, which are enforced for credit reference agencies who decide whether someone can buy furniture on HP, are far more important for records which determine the provision of an enormous range of social and financial benefits, and the employment prospects of millions of people.

---

(1) *Oldham Evening Chronicle,* 19 June 1975

(2) *Confidentiality in Social Work,* British Association of Social Workers (undated), para 1.4

(3) *New Society,* 8 February 1973

(4) *Community Care,* 23 May 1975

(5) *Confidentiality in Social Work,* Appendix II

(6) *A Study of the Computing Requirements of Local Government in England,* Local Authorities Management Services and Computer Committee (undated)

(7) Law Commission Working Papers 56: *Conspiracy to Defraud,* HMSO 1974

Education

School pupils and their parents are familiar with the end of term report, often providing only minimal information about the child's progress. But most of them do not realise that the school maintains a second, secret record on the child, which is transferred with the child from primary to secondary school, and which may include a mixture of facts about the child, reports on the family situation and teachers' opinions and theories about both.

These confidential records are, of course, supposed to benefit the child by ensuring that each teacher involved with the child will have adequate information about the child's background. The reality is less reassuring. A contributor to Education *Guardian*[1] spent some time examining, with the help of cooperative teachers, the confidential records of a number of schools — records which often turned out to be 'tatty bits of paper bearing illegible scrawls'. Many LEAs, however, provide standard record cards, to ensure that information and views are more efficiently recorded. Forty-three LEA's provided sample record cards in response to a survey by the Advisory Centre for Education magazine, *Where,* in October 1975. One such card asks the teacher to indicate, on a scale of 1 to 10, how a child rates on a series of attributes, including honesty, leadership, truthfulness and sycophamcy!

Such records are begun in primary school, although in Coventry a new record system, involving more than 130 questions has been introduced in selected 'infants' schools. One record, seen by NCCL, followed the child through a number of years and included the following remarks:

> 'Mother says she's nervous and highly strung. I think this could be inherited from mother. A bit concerned over S.'s honesty — though as yet have no evidence . . .
>
> 'Still brings in dolls, trinkets etc from home which she allows other children to 'borrow' for the day. (Buying popularity?) . . .
>
> 'She needs a tremendous amount of attention and is demanding towards Y., the drama advisor (sp!), she shows possessiveness — he must sit by her, read the book she's brought etc. . . . She also shows this attitude towards other males — and yet she's not at all coy . . .
>
> 'Not convinced she always tells the complete truth: mum came round one evening and made one or two remarks that were not fully accurate.
>
> 'Not a popular girl.'

Such pseudo-psychological comments (is S. supposed to have 'inherited' her mother's nervousness or merely imitated it), or the extraordinary assumption that a child should be blamed for a mother's inaccuracies should never be allowed to remain unchallenged in a permanent record. Another report recorded that one of the boy pupils was showing an unusual interest in sex and had dirty sexual habits. The teacher commented that he always looked for pictures of women to use in projects. The child had once been found exposing himself in the school playground. He was aged 10.

Woman magazine, in an article on school records, quoted a letter from a teacher and acting headmaster, who said of a young girl's record; 'I once felt it needful to cut out the words: 'This girl is a thief and a liar and shy' from the card of a girl who during her sojourn with us (while I was both her class teacher and the acting head) proved honest, truthful, frank and extremely helpful at all times.'

The deputy head of a comprehensive school was astonished to find, on a record card for a pupil who had recently transferred from primary school, the following comment: (a) From infancy has been a tomboy. (b) Tomboyish, never wears a dress, always boyish clothes. (c) Very much a tomboy — latest interest is motorbikes!' The comment was written in the space headed 'Significant medical information.'

Serious injustice may be done to a child by a false record card. In one case brought to NCCL's attention, a 15-year-old boy was accused by someone else at his school of attacking a younger boy, and demanding money from him. Although the headteacher told the father that his son was not involved, both the 15-year-old and his younger brother were subjected to abuse at school. The children were transferred to another school in the same area, and when the father went to see the new headmaster, it turned out that the alleged theft had gone down on the boy's records. Nor had the information been kept confidential: a new teacher who asked the younger boy if they were brothers, commented 'Oh, the thief'. The father complained to his local MP, the LEA and the Home Secretary, but got no satisfactory result.

The knowledge that secret records exist, and are used as the basis for references to employers and colleges, can inhibit pupils' freedom of action. NCCL's women's rights officer received a letter from a number of girls at a mixed comprehensive, complaining of discrimination in their school and asking for advice. They were happy to talk to anyone about their complaints — but said that they couldn't have any publicity in case it affected what the headmaster put in their files.

The *Where* survey discovered that virtually every LEA keeps such records confidential, although 24 were prepared to grant access on a discretionary basis. In April 1976, the Inner London Education Authority decided to open primary school records to parents. Clwyd and Dorset LEAs also keep open records, although the Campaign against Secret Records on Schoolchildren reports that one parent in Dorset was not in fact allowed to see the child's record. Disclosure of a record can also be compelled in a court case: in July 1976, the High Court rejected a claim by the ILEA that it should not have to disclose its records on a schoolboy who was alleged to have injured another pupil. The records were wanted by the injured pupil's parents, who wanted to claim damages against the authority.[2]

The National Consumer Council have published a draft Code of Practice[3] — backed by the Advisory Centre for Education, the Confederation for the Advancement of State Education, the National Association of Governors and Managers and the National Union of School Students — which proposes that 'the LEA and the school should be expected to allow ready access to parents and pupils to all personal records relating to them, and to be prepared to justify fully any exception to this right to know.' the NCC argue cogently that inaccurate information or mistaken impressions cannot be corrected unless parents can see the pupil's records, and that, for the same reason, pupils too should be able to see their own file. (Rather than have an arbitrary age at which pupils could see their records, it might be preferable to have a procedure which is sufficiently flexible to allow older primary-school children, as well as all secondary pupils, to see their file if they wished.) The NCC stress that the argument that a pupil might be disturbed by discovering some previously unknown fact about the family is 'outweighed by the more general danger of misrepresentation', and that any exceptional need to conceal the record from the child should be agreed between the parent and the school.

In the United States, the Buckley Act, passed at the end of 1974, gives parents and students the right to see their own or their child's files.[4] The Act applies to the present and former students of any public school or college, and some private ones as well. Students aged 18 or over exercise their rights directly; the files on those under 18 are opened to the parents. A teacher's private notes, provided they are not placed on a permanent record, are exempt from disclosure, as are medical or psychiatric records on students aged 18 or over which are used in connection with medical treatment and are only available to professionals involved in the treatment. References and letters of recommendation written after 1 January 1975 are open for inspection, although the student may waive this right. The Act provides a right for students to challenge 'inaccurate, misleading or otherwise inappropriate' entries in their records, and specifies that information must not be passed on to a third party without the student's consent. (There is, however, an exception to the need for consent where records are being transferred to another school, or opened to certain state or federal authorities.) Finally, each school or college must keep a record of everyone requesting access to the student's records and the reason why the request was granted. This record, along with the rest of the file, is made available to the parent or student.

Further and higher education

Just as the file passed from primary to secondary school may have devastating effects on the pupil, so the letter sent from secondary school to a college, polytechnic or university can destroy a student's hope of a place. Where, for instance, university entrance is decided before A-level results are known, the head teacher's prediction of the results is a crucial factor in the decision. Students who have been politically active at school may get adverse reports sent to a prospective college. The reference sent from university or college to a prospective employer may — as the case on page 58 shows — come as a very nasty shock, when allegations or criticisms that were never made openly to the student are written down for the benefit of an employer. Students in occupations in a number of colleges have discovered files containing extremely subjective and unsubstantiated comments about individuals.

A Buckley Act is needed here to give students the right to see their own references and records, challenge their accuracy, and control any transfer outside the institution. There is also a need for a time-limit to be placed on the storage of records after students leave. At one university which was considering computerising records, members of the committee discussing suitable procedures proposed a series of measures to safeguard the students' privacy; the result of the discussion was to make some tutors question the value of keeping records at all, and the proposal was made to destroy all records 5 years after the student graduates.

The aims of the Campaign Against Secret Records on School Children apply equally to school and higher education records. The Campaign wants to see all reports compiled by properly trained observers, with proper checking procedures; they should be regularly updated and should not contain any 'psuedo-scientific jargon'; parents or the students themselves should have a legal right to see the report; there should be legal safeguards on the transfer of information to outside bodies; and parents or students should have the right to add their own comments to the files. Consumers have the right to add explanatory notes to a credit reference file; parents and students have an even more pressing need to be able to see and correct an educational record.

Lecturers themselves are also the victims of secrecy. Students in an occupation at Exeter University came across a list of 30 lecturers, kept in the files of the Vice-Chancellor. The names were divided into three categories: 'politically left and generally anti-establishment'; 'bright personalities with no particular affiliation; not really Establishment types occasionally a bit aggressive'; and 'awkward'. The Vice-Chancellor is reported to have said that the list was given to him in answer to a request for information about members of the university who might participate in a series of lunch-time lectures.[5]) As we argue in the section on employment, employees should have a right to inspect and challenge personnel records, although in most cases they would not be able to sue for libel.

---

(1) *Guardian* 30 March 1976

(2) *Times* 31 July 1976

(3) *Advise and Consent,* Proposals for a Code of Practice; National Consumer Council, February 1977

(4) For more information on the Buckley Act, see the *Privacy Report* (American Civil Liberties Union) Vol II, No 4, February 1975; and *Your School Records,* Children's Defense Fund, Washington DC, March 1976

(5) *Guardian,* 8 March 1977

Medical records

> 'Whatsoever things I see or hear concerning the life of men, in my attendance on the sick or even apart therefrom, which ought not to be noised abroad, I will keep silence thereon, counting such things to be as sacred secrets'.

For over 2,000 years, the Hippocratic Oath has committed doctors to respecting the confidences of their patients. How many people realise that secrets entrusted to their doctor are shared with a growing circle of professionals, researchers, civil servants and other third parties over whom neither doctor nor patient has any control?

Medical privacy is vital for two reasons. Firstly, it is a basic human right to control information about oneself. The transfer of medical information to a third party without the patient's informed consent infringes this right. The second reason is a practical one. Unless the patient has complete confidence in the doctor's willingness and ability to respect privacy, he or she may not give the doctor all the information — intimate and embarrassing though it may be — which is needed for proper diagnosis and treatment. Any threat to medical privacy undermines the basis of the medical relationship itself.

This stress on confidentiality raises conflicts which may be difficult to resolve.[1] Should a doctor involve a third party where, for instance, a patient is threatening suicide? Should a doctor who suspects that a child has been injured by the parents keep silent, and risk harm to the child, or break confidence with the parents who brought the child to the doctor, and tell the police or local authority? Should a doctor tell the employers where a worker is found to be suffering from a serious condition which could jeopardise other people's lives (a bus driver, for instance, suffering from a heart condition)? If the police, in search of a multiple rapist, discover that the suspect suffers from a medical condition shared by only a small proportion of adult males, should they be able to force a doctor to search his records in order to identify possible suspects?[2]

Well-founded public concern about injured children has focussed attention on the creation of 'at risk' registers and the need for close cooperation between social workers, the police, doctors and hospital authorities — a co-operation which inevitably involves sharing information which one worker may have initially received in confidence. On the face of it, there cannot be serious objections to the doctor passing on information about a child who is apparently being injured by the parents: the child, after all, is the doctor's patient, as well as the parents. But there are serious objections where the doctor conveys his suspicions to a third party without either telling the parents what is being done, or at least ensuring that the parents know that they are now suspected baby batterers. In the section on social work records (see page 24), we point out that parents suspected of battering can suffer most serious consequences, without there being initially any proper trial of the evidence which forms the basis for the suspicion. Not only do the parents have a right to know that they are under suspicion and why; a good doctor or social worker may be able, if they are honest with the parents, to help them look after their child.

The conflict between confidentiality and some other social interest is not, of course, confined to doctors. In the case of Patrick Meehan, imprisoned for a crime of which he was not guilty, another man had confessed to his solicitor that he was in fact guilty of the murder. Rather than break a professional confidence and jeopardise the confidential relationship between client and solicitor, the solicitor remained silent about the confession until his client died.

All the professional groups involved in medical care — doctors, nurses, social workers, psychiatrists, clinical psychologists and so on — have well-established ethical standards which place considerable emphasis on confidentiality. Nonetheless, the patient's privacy is increasingly abused as information given to one person for one purpose is placed in central data banks, transferred to other departments and shared with other workers. A report by the Royal College of Psychiatrists in 1976 referred to the worrying absence of any uniform procedure for ensuring the confidentiality of hospital case-notes: in some hospitals, only doctors and their secretaries read the notes; in others, they are available to social workers, nurses, clinical psychologists, occupational therapists and students; in others again, any member of staff may read them. 'Quite apart from what is supposed to happen,' the report comments, 'in some hospitals security is so lax that patients and casual visitors can easily pick up and read 'confidential' case notes.'

The following letter to NCCL illustrates the distress which can be caused by the transfer of medical records:

> 'I have been seeing my GP recently about my daughter's emotional problems, and he now holds a psychiatric report on my daughter which contains references to myself. Recently I mentioned to him that as my daughter was outgrowing her difficulties I would wish to have her notes destroyed when she leaves his care, but I was told that on re-registration notes are automatically forwarded to the new GP and that this is outside the patient's control. A second problem is that my daughter . . . may well become a boarder. In this case, her notes would be kept at the school, thereby giving the matron and headmistress access to confidential information, not only about my daughter but about myself as well . . . My own view is that any information which I have given to my doctor is strictly between that particular doctor and myself, should be regarded as completely confidential and should not be divulged to *anybody* without my consent . . . This is causing me a great deal of personal distress as I do not feel able to talk to my doctor as long as my conversations are virtually public.'

It used to be commonly reported that a GP, when asked for contraceptives by a girl aged under 16, had informed the parents without her consent.

Although the DHSS, in a circular to GPs, has suggested that they should not inform the parents unless the girl has agreed, the final decision is still left to the GP. As a result, many girls continue to be terrified of going to a local GP for fear their privacy will not be respected.

Because it is illegal for a man to have intercourse with a girl under 16 — although the law is rarely enforced in practice — the police may also become involved in cases involving young girls. A doctor reported to NCCL that he had diagnosed a concealed pregnancy in a young girl, who was about 36 weeks pregnant.

> 'She and her mother were insistent that the pregnancy should be kept as much of a secret as possible. They wanted an adoption arranged. I made an appointment at the next clinic with the local consultant obstetrician and arranged for the girl to be seen by the welfare officer with a view to arranging adoption of the infant. . . . A woman police officer phoned asking for a certificate of the girl's pregnancy. Mother said that the welfare officer had phoned the police and the child's headmistress. The police had insisted on statements from the child and her mother and had threatened examination by a police doctor if I refused to supply a certificate. . . . I have had a conversation with the welfare officer concerned. She is employed by (a voluntary organisation) and says that she is legally obliged to inform the police of any pregnancy occurring in a girl under the age of 15 and that this is the policy laid down by her head office. I have also phoned a senior social worker who is involved in the case and he has said it is not his policy to bring the police in on these cases unless there is a complaint by the girl or the parents of rape.'

Not only does this case illustrate the disturbing consequences of involving the police in a matter which was essentially private; it also shows clearly the number of people likely to become involved in caring for a patient. Within a few days of the initial visit to the family doctor — when mother and daughter stressed their wish for secrecy — news of the pregnancy had been shared with a welfare officer, the police, the girl's headmistress and the local social work department.

Nor is this the only situation where the police may obtain confidential medical information. The same doctor complained to NCCL when, towards the end of 1975, he received two circular letters from his Family Practitioner Committee in Essex, inviting him to contact the police if the people named approached him as patients. The first circular gave the name of a woman, a permanent address (said to be false) and her temporary address, going on to say:

> 'The Committee has been informed that the above named patient may be approaching doctors as a temporary resident in the area endeavouring to obtain prescriptions for high doses of tranquillisers, sleeping tables including Valium 10.
>
> 'The patient appears unwashed of a 'hippy type', approximately 5' 10" tall, wears long skirt, shirt and shawl. The patient may

> state that she is three months pregnant.
>
> 'If such a person approaches you for a prescription, it would be appreciated if you would inform the local police.'

The second circular gave the patient's name and an address, also described as false, stating that the patient had been removed from his doctor's list.

> 'It is also understood that the patient is described as being small, aged about 25 years, as having unkempt blonde hair (possibly bleached), of untidy appearance, hippy type, but reasonably clean. The patient has used the names of .... and ....
>
> 'Should the patient approach you for a supply of Ritalin you are asked, if possible, to retain him and inform the local police.'

Not only did the circulars invite doctors to breach medical confidentiality in approaching the police, but the second clearly suggested that the doctor should simplify the police's job by arresting the patient for them. Since the doctor complained to the Family Practitioner Committee about such circulars, he stopped receiving them and it seems that this particular FPC has ceased the practice of asking GPs to contact the local police.

Another GP has complained to NCCL about similar circulars from his Family Practitioner Committee, warning him about people who might try to obtain supplies of drugs although not asking him to contact the police. He pointed out that the circulars were in practice useless, since he had no recall system which would allow him to match up the given name and description with an individual who might come to his surgery months later.

The Abortion (Amendment) Bill, introduced by William Benyon MP in 1977 would have given the police a new power to apply for a search warrant, allowing them to inspect and copy any document held by an agency providing pregnancy tests, counselling or abortions. The power would not apply to NHS hospitals. Thus, any woman attending a charitable or commercial clinic or advisory agency would do so at risk of losing all hope of confidentiality. Although the Bill fell at the end of the Parliamentary Session, a similar clause may well find its way into new measures designed to restrict the availability of abortion.

The case quoted earlier of the 13-year-old girl illustrated the way in which a multi-disciplinary approach depends on increased sharing of information. MIND, in its evidence to the Data Protection Committee, refers to the implications for mentally ill patients.

> 'But the prevention of mental ill health and its care and treatment crosses a number of administrative boundaries so that there is an increasing tendency for information to be passed not merely between one professional and another but between different national and local government agencies including health authorities, social services, general practitioner services, housing, education, supplementary benefits and even the police. Inevitably such information can be used for the purposes of social control of rent defaulters, child abusers, adopters and foster parents, and recipients of supplementary benefits.

Where information is shared — particularly where it is shared with workers who do not have a professional code enjoining them to respect confidentiality — the need for measures to protect the individual become even more apparent. A doctor giving evidence to the United States Senate Subcommittee on Privacy reported the case of a young woman who went to a neighbourhood health centre, complaining of tiredness, loss of appetitie, and overdue period. The doctor decided on a pregnancy test as part of a full examination. The woman's next-door neighbour worked as a typist in the centre and noticed that a pregnancy test was being performed. Soon the neighbourhood knew that the woman was suspected of being pregnant and, finally, her parents were told. Forced to leave the community, the woman committed suicide. The autopsy confirmed that she was a virgin and that the overdue periods were a consequence of hyperthyroidism.[3])

It is not only those involved in the care of a patient who may acquire confidential information. An employer may require an employee or job applicant to undergo a medical test; questionnaires used for this purpose can include searching questions about the applicant's family as well as the applicant (see page 52 for an example). Although the doctor is professionally bound not to give medical details to the employer, the employer — who is not bound by medical ethics — will be told general conclusions about the applicant's or employee's fitness. An insurance company receives detailed information on someone taking out life or disability insurance, or a private patient applying for insurance or making a claim. The DHSS maintains information on workers claiming national insurance benefit during illness; and collects information from doctors, for statistical purposes, about an employee's illness which led to a national insurance claim, but where no diagnosis appeared on the certificate (e.g. for a hospital patient). The DHSS states that it is entirely in the doctor's discretion whether to supply the information requested and whether to seek the patient's consent for doing so.

The most disturbing aspect of the increasing flow of medical information from doctor or psychiatrist to a range of other workers and agencies is that information recorded for one purpose, or a judgement made by one professional only, will follow the patient throughout his or her life, forming the basis for a series of adverse judgements. For instance, a school may be informed that a child is 'hyper active', a 'slow learner' or 'disturbed'. The consequences were described by the Assistant Commissioner for Drug Rehabilitation in Massachussets:

> 'A doctor's decision that a child is a slow learner or 'hyper-active' will follow that child throughout his or her school career. It will influence teacher attitudes and expectations which will, in turn, program that very behaviour in the child even if *the original perception by the physician was false or capricious.* Significant changes in IQ can actually be measured as a function of teacher expectation. Children mistakenly diagnosed as hyper-active have been kept on amphetamines or ritalin throughout their development years with unknown long-term consequences. Physicians have informed

teachers that children perceived as having reading difficulty will in many cases be seen as having psychiatric difficulties several years later. This is justified in terms of 'early case finding' and 'preventive intervention' but serves only to convince the teacher that any difficulty children have in learning is a function of a serious defect in the student rather than in the school or the teacher himself, which is more often the case.'[4])

Much of the 'information' recorded about a patient is essentially a subjective judgment by the psychiatrist, social worker or doctor involved. It may well be helpful for the individual worker to record, on the notes he or she keeps, his or her own opinion of the patient. It is a very different matter for such a judgment to be recorded in an information retrieval system to which a number of other workers will have access. As MIND says, 'subjective judgments may easily be wrong or ill informed but in the hands of a practitioner who is not in the first instance responsible for making such judgments and who does not have the benefit of a personal relationship with the person concerned, they can become highly damaging.' A note added to a file, or an opinion expressed at a case conference, is recognisable as an individual judgment; the same view, transferred to a computerised data bank, may acquire the status of a fact, divorced from the personality or qualifications of the person making the judgment or the circumstances in which it was made. Both NCCL and MIND have stressed that subjective judgments should not be included in any data bank system.

Psychiatric records

Psychiatric records, which may contain intimate and embarrassing details about someone's life, require the most stringent measures to protect confidentiality. But in 1976, the Royal College of Psychiatrists protested about the 'disturbing and deteriorating situation' with psychiatric records. Records are usually held in a psychiatric hospital by a central medical records department, with current case notes kept on the ward. Copies of the records are often requested by other hospitals or doctors, solicitors, the police and government departments. Since notes made in an NHS hospital belong, not to the doctor who makes them, or the patient about whom the notes are made, but to the Department of Health, a copy may be demanded by any senior DHSS official. Some hospitals send copies, others refuse to do so; but there is no national policy on disclosure, and often the doctors — like the patients — have no idea of what happens to 'confidential' records. The College also points out that any organisation which gets a copy of a record can copy it, reducing even the minimal standards of security which obtained for the original. The College comments 'it is most doubtful that any patient would ever give consent for this procedure if he knew of the situation.'

The College has proposed that every hospital, and especially every psychiatric hospital, should have a Medical Records Committee, including doctors, nurses and the records officer, to take responsibility for the security and confidentiality of records. They also recommend that, where case-notes are widely available, the amount of information recorded should be reduced; that information obtained for one purpose should not be transferred for another purpose without consent; and that psychiatrists who obtain 'intimate, shameful or legally damaging facts' about a patient should consider carefully whether this information needs to be recorded and, if so, should use a private phrase as a reminder of certain facts or maintain a separate filing system under the psychiatrist's own direct control.

Medical Data Banks

The three largest medical data banks — the National Health Service Registers for England and Wales, Scotland and Northern Ireland — are operated manually, although they will be computerised in the future. They contain information about everyone who has ever registered with an NHS doctor and, patients who have died, emigrated or joined the Armed Forces, and are used by Family Practitioner Committee to maintain GPs' patient lists, allocate new NHS numbers and deal with requests for transfers to another doctor. Where a prospective patient cannot quote an NHS number and is not clearly registering with a GP for the first time, the patient is asked for information about date of birth, previous addresses, parents' name and mother's maiden name and, for someone who has come from abroad, passport number and date of entry into the United Kingdom.

Regional Health Authorities throughout the UK also maintain a number of computerised systems, using information supplied by GPs and hospitals. For instance, a GP carrying out a cervical smear test has to provide details of the woman's name and maiden name, address, husband's occupation (and whether 'manager, foreman or other'), marital status, number of pregnancies and abortions, details of symptoms and the results of the test. The information is coded and a serial number allocated to the patient's name. It is then used for research, aimed at indentifying causes of cervical cancer.

In England and Wales, each of the fourteen Regional Authorities maintains a computerised Hospital Activity Analysis (HAA) which was started in 1970. Whenever a patient leaves hospital, a clerk transfers to the HAA data bank the patient's name and address, details of the medical condition and treatment, information about marital status, occupation and religion, and, for abortion cases, details of previous pregnancies. Information about different visits to hospital is not, except in the case of the Oxford Linkage Study, connected, so that a patient who is discharged from hospital twice in a year appears twice on the computer records. But the Oxford Study is designed to link all records from hospitals in the Oxford region about the same person, and to connect them with birth and death records, and eventually to information from GPs. In order to make the connections, each person is assigned a number, and a separate index file links name and number by matching up not only the name, but also sex, date of b sometimes address, NHS number and place of birth. In something under 1% of the cases, the files of two different people are wrongly linked together.

The Oxford Study has met with objections from practitioners in Aylesbury, who are quite prepared to co-operate in supplying non-identifiable medical information but who have refused to supply names and addresses.[5]

The chairman of the medical advisory committee which took the decision to withhold names and addresses four years ago when the Linkage Study was extended to Aylesbury, is seriously concerned by the breach of medical confidence involved in handing over not only medical details, but also information about a patient's social background, without the patient's knowledge or consent. He also points to the danger of incorrect data — arising either from the inaccurate linkages made in a small proportion of cases, or from errors made by the clerk who fills out the HAA form on the basis of the consultant's discharge report. Such errors, while statistically insignificant, could be extremely serious if decisions were made about individuals on the basis of the computer records.

In the absence of any statutory safeguards, some doctors also fear that computerised medical data could be linked with social service, criminal or other records, and used for political or other purposes which the doctor and patient have no control over. Since the police already ask GPs to inform them about patients who may be police suspects, the danger of a complete linking of medical and criminal records is not remote.

The HAA, dealing with patients discharged from hospital, is parallelled by the Mental Health Enquiry, a computerised data-bank on psychiatric in-patients which is operated by the DHSS. Information on mental patients includes details of epilepsy, drug dependency and alcoholism, and whether the patient was referred by the police or the courts. Although the DHSS allows hospitals to omit the address and religion, which are not computerised the patient's name is included. But doctors in Aylesbury have now begun to omit the name, as well as address, from the MHE forms, and the DHSS has apparently continued to use the information and make statistical abstracts (on bed use and so on) available to the Aylesbury hospitals. By contrast, the Oxford Records Linkage Study has refused to accept un-named data for its HAA records.

The Royal College of Psychiatrists has accepted, in connection with the Mental Health Enquiry, that 'medical information obtained about individual patients should continue to be made available without their explicit consent for the purpose of medical research', despite the fact that information about psychiatric patients is even more sensitive — and potentially more damaging, if revealed — than information about other patients. There is, of course, a strong case for making information about patients available for research purposes. Sometimes, however, this can be done by asking the doctor or hospital to provide the necessary information about symptoms, treatment, family background and so on, *without* giving the name and address. This could, for instance, be done in the study of cervical smear tests mentioned earlier. Where the name and other identifying material are needed, as in the Oxford Linkage Study, the patient must be asked to consent to the transfer of information and proper safeguards must be built into the system. In particular, the index file, used to connect the individual patient with the anonymous information abstracted for statistical or research purposes, should be kept separately from the research material itself. Thus, those who have access to the medical and social information would not also be able to have access to the index enabling them to link records to an individual. This cannot be achieved while records remain the property, not of the doctor or patient, but the Secretary of State for Health, without even the supervision of a Data Protection Authority.

Medical research and the compilation of statistics raises the question of whether the researchers should be able to initiate further contact with the individual subjects of the study. If, for instance, the researchers conclude that certain patients — identified to them only by serial numbers — are in a high risk category for a particular condition, or if they need more information, should they be able to search the index file in order to identify and contact those people? Since contact between the researchers and the individuals would — for however benign a purpose — breach the undertakings of confidentiality which should have been given at the outset, we would suggest that any follow-up should be made, not by the researchers, but by the independent body holding the link file, who could notify the patient's doctor.

Separation of the index file and the detailed information about each individual does not remove the possibility that a court would order disclosure of information — for instance, in the situation described earlier, where a suspect in a serious criminal case is known to suffer from a comparatively rare condition. This danger could be minimised by keeping the index link out of the country — a safeguard used by an education data bank in the United States, which keeps the index in Canada — thus ensuring that the data bank in this country would be physically unable to supply information about named individuals.

In addition to Regional Health Authority and DHSS records, a number of NHS hospitals maintain their own computers, for instance for scheduling in — and out-patients, organising nurse rotas, keeping maternity records, compiling statistics of patients, treatments, staff records and so on. There have also been experiments on the use of computers to store full personal medical records. It has therefore become possible for many hospitals to store an enormous range of information about those who come either as in-patients or for out-patients treatment. A hospital patient visiting an out-patient clinic at a Middlesex hospital was asked to complete a 4-page questionnaire, which included questions not only about her past and present medical problems and treatment (one page), but also details of her own and her husband's occupation, field of business and social-economic status; accommodiation details (including number of bedrooms); smoking and drinking habits; the age, medical history and whether alive or dead for both parents, spouse, sisters, brothers and children; hereditary conditions; travel outside Britain in the last two years; travel or

Hospital and social services re-organisation has increased the likelihood that detailed personal information will be widely shared. In evidence to the Data Protection Committee, MIND pointed out that: 'Now that psychiatric hospital-based social workers have been incorporated in the local authority social services structure the transfer and therefore the wider availability of personal information has become inevitable. Social services departments themselves are frequently called upon to give information to other local authority departments, like education and housing, and in some areas there is an automatic transfer of information to the police and juvenile bureau.'

Since 1971, a pilot scheme in West Sussex has involved computerising school health, vaccination and immunisation, early child health and education department records within the local authority's computer system, and to link all the records on an individual child by a link file containing 'non-confidential identifying data'.6) The system should reduce clerical work, improve liaison between different agencies, allow for the preparation of registers of pupils with special conditions, and provide statistical information for Central Government and research. Medical information will also be given to the Youth Careers Service. A record will be kept on each child up until he or she leaves school, when a summary will then be sent to the family doctor. 'A similar summary will be stored on tape against subsequent enquiries and the possibility of future medical record linkage.' The memorandum describing the scheme does not say what these 'enquiries' might be; nor is there any proposal to inform parents or pupils of the new scheme, or seek their approval for the transfer of information between different departments.

One of the main effects of computerisation is that it enables a very large number of people to have easy access to detailed information which was previously kept in card index boxes or filing cabinets. It is therefore especially important to restrict the number of people who need to have access to the information, to limit the information they can see, and to ensure that unauthorised people (or those authorised to see only part of the file) cannot see the full record. In Sweden, the central data-bank in Stockholm has classified medical information into three categories according to sensitivity. The most sensitive category includes psychiatric records and information on VD and gynaecological problems. People who use the data-bank are given codes which provide access to particular grades of confidential information. The problem with such an approach is that general categories cannot always protect the individual: for instance, while details of contraceptive provision may only be of 'medium-grade' sensitivity for most people, keeping them secret may be of highest importance to an unmarried Catholic woman. Nevertheless, it is essential to build into any computerised medical data-bank a coding system which limits access to the smallest number of people possible.

It is clear from this brief review that medical data-banks do not satisfy the standards laid down in the Government's own White Paper.7) Firstly, the White Paper states that 'the existence and purpose' of information systems should be publicly known, together with the kind of information they handle and the use they make of the information. While the accompanying report[8] on public sector data-banks refers to medical data-banks and lists the 'tasks' performed by hospital computers, it omits to mention the crucial Oxford Linkage Study, does not give the number of hospital computerised data-banks nor which hospitals use them, and provides such elliptical information about proposed medical uses of computers (e.g. 'patient monitoring, clinical measurement and nuclear medicine system', 'clinical decision-making systems') that a non-medical reader cannot identify the kind of information involved, nor the use made of it, while even a medical reader would not know how widespread such systems were. Indeed, it was discovered in Aylesbury that very few doctors knew that data on psychiatric patients was being collected.

Secondly, the White Paper states that information given for one purpose should not be used for another without either the individual's consent or some other 'authorised justification'. The patient whose medical and social history is being data banked usually has no idea of what will happen to the information given to the doctor for the purpose of securing treatment. Very often the doctor has no knowledge of the secondary purpose for which this information is being gathered. The justification claimed for medical data banks is the need for better research into health conditions in order to ensure better care in future, and the more efficient use of resources and provision of services. But the authority for using personal information for research should come from the patient, not the DHSS.

The White Paper also states that, in general, statistics should not reveal details of an identified or identifiable individual. Although published statistics do not, of course, do so, it is questionable whether individuals need to be identified at any stage of the research process. The DHSS allows hospitals to delete name and address from the Hospital Activity Analysis in most parts of the country, but the Oxford Linkage Study depends on a name-number index which is not kept separately from the main data bank. In the Mental Health Enquiry, doctors are permitted to delete the name of the patient, although only about 5% do so. It should not be for the DHSS or the Regional Health Authorities to decide what doctors should disclose or what they may be permitted to conceal: Parliament should legislate for safeguards designed to restore control of personal information to the individual.

Allowing patients to see their records

Medical records, especially on hospital patients, are likely to be shared amongst doctors, nurses, secretaries, administrative workers, other medical workers, social workers, DHSS officials and even the police — depending on the policy of the particular institution. The one person who is barred from seeing his or her 'confidential' record is the patient. There are three occasions when the patient may in fact see the record. Some doctors allow their patients to look at the notes. Some hospitals appear to be so lax in their security procedures that the patient (along with any casual visitor) can pick up the file and have a look. And a patient considering an action for negligence can instruct a solicitor who will get access to the records, and may show them to the client, while medical records may also be obtained in other legal actions (e.g. a divorce case).

Isn't it time that the patient was added to the list of those who have a legitimate right to see medical case-notes and records? The essential case for allowing the patient access to his or her record is no different from the case for access to any other file: access is required in the interests of individual privacy; as a matter of ordinary fairness to the subject of the record; and as a practical method of ensuring that inaccuracies and irrelvancies may be challenged. But somehow it is felt that allowing people to see their own medical records would be dangerous. In particular, it is argued that someone might discover he or she was suffering from a fatal illness. This last objection conceals a far more important issue: the inability of many doctors to treat a dying patient honestly. Many transfer the responsibility of deciding whether or not to tell the dying person by telling the nearest relative. The risk that a patient might brutally discover the truth by looking at his case-notes might force doctors to face up to their responsibility by explaining the situation to the patient themselves. It has also been suggested, however, that patients are able to protect themselves from definite information in such cases and should not therefore be denied access.[9]

It may also be argued that patients suffering from mental illness would not benefit from seeing their own record. But MIND, in its evidence to the Data Protection Committee, says that it is 'not convinced that mental health records require the degree of divergence from general principles recommended by some practitioners . . . . An exception (to disclosure to the individual) could be made for information which in the opinion of the practitioner concerned could damage the health or severely curtail the treatment programme of the individual concerned. If such an exception is to be made the practitioner should be subjected to a system of accountability which involves placing an explanation on record at the time the decision is reached . . . Wherever possible some other person representing the interests of the individual concerned should be informed, be this a nearest relative or a guardian. We would add that the case for exceptions is not, in our view, particularly strong.'

We do not believe that any of the arguments advanced in favour of keeping records secret from patients can outweigh the fundamental arguments in favour of a general rule which gives people the right to know what is being written on their record.

---

(1) 'Ethical Aspects of Medical Confidentiality', Le Roy Walters Ph D, Director, Centre for Bioethics, Kennedy Institute, Washington DC; in United States Senate Joint Hearings on Privacy, Part II, 1974

(2) The Cambridge rapist apparently suffered from a condition shared by less than 5% of the adult male population – non-emission at orgasm. The proposal was made – and rejected – for a search of local doctors' records in order to identify men with this condition.

(3) Evidence by Dr E Gabrieli, chairman, Joint Task Force on Ethical Health Data Centres; US Senate Subcommittee on Privacy 1974, Part I, page 349

(4) US Senate Subcommittee on Privacy 1974, Part I, page 559

(5) *New Scientist* 5 July 1973 and 29 July 1976

(6) *A Computer-assisted Scheme for the School Health Service,* West Sussex County Council, July 1972

(7) Cmnd 6353, para 34

(8) Cmnd 6354

(9) J McIntosh, *Lancet,* 7 August 1976, page 300.

Employment

Should employers be entitled to obtain detailed information about an applicant's private life? Should they be able to pass on opinions about a worker or ex-employee who has no way of knowing what is being said or challenging its accuracy? Should personnel records and references be so 'confidential' that the individual subject of the record has no right to see them?

Government departments, local authorities and other public sector employees are well known for the detailed questions asked of job applicants, usually with the threat that concealment or false replies will lead to dismissal. The East Sussex County Council application form includes a Health Statement, where the candidate is required to list all previous operations, injuries or serious illnesses; whether s/he has ever suffered from, amongst other things, 'nervous or mental disease'; and whether any of the family have suffered from mental illness. A letter from the County Council states that, according to the area medical officer, 'no medical screen is complete without information about the family's (health) history and that he would be quite unable to proffer any advice to the County Council as the prospective employers without this information.' There are at present no legal controls about how long such information can be kept if the applicant obtains the job, whether it is destroyed when the applicant is unsuccessful or whether it can be used in subsequent references or performance reviews.

An application form used by Lothian Council in 1975, headed 'Medical Assessment', also asked for information about family medical history as well as details of the applicant's own medical condition. But in addition, it required applicants to state whether they ever smoked ' 'cannabis,' 'hash', 'pot' etc' or had ever been treated for any illness connected with alcohol or drugs. The Scottish Council for Civil Liberties took the matter up with the Council who agreed to review the form.

A Post Office application form includes questions about the present and past nationality of mother, father and spouse; whether the spouse has a different address from the applicant; details of any mental illness suffered; the applicant's citizenship, how acquired, and any past citizenship; whether the applicant is a citizen of the Irish Republic by birth; any previous convictions (including probation, absolute or conditional discharges and binding over orders); and any outstanding summons or charges (including motoring, but not parking offences). The form states that a 'yes' answer to the questions on convictions or charges does not necessarily bar the applicant from employment, since 'every case is considered on its merits'.

Similarly, a Department of Education and Science form for would-be schools inspectors requests the names and maiden names, present or last address, present and previous nationalities and occupation of the applicant's father, mother and spouse.

In some cases, information is needed in order to meet statutory requirements — for instance, that schools inspectors be British subjects who can either show that one of his or her parents was also a British subject or who meets certain residence requirements.

Information required by some private employers is often more searching than that needed by the Civil Service, and cannot be justified by the demands of the job. Niagara Finance, a Canadian firm, supplied a four-page form to someone looking for work with the UK division in 1974. The form included the following questions:

> dates of marriage, separation, divorce, remarriage;
> the health of children and other dependants (in one line);
> 'have you any worries as to disposition, habits, appearance, health etc?'
> 'explain any unemployment period longer than 30 days';
> father's and mother's 'outstanding personality traits or characteristics';
> 'are you like him or her?'
> 'in regard to your problems, were (are) your parents sympathetic and understanding?
> 'was your life at home a happy one?'
> 'is your wife (sic) working?'
> 'what are your hobbies?'
> 'describe what you do each evening of a typical week'
> 'what things have caused you most humiliation or sense of failure?'

The form adds that any misrepresentation in any of the statements on the form will be cause for dismissal, and that the form will be used as a permanent record for an employee. Although the company state that this form has been withdrawn, they still demand detailed information about family background and interests etc. NCCL receives frequent complaints from people who object to the personal nature of some questions asked by prospective employers. Someone who refuses to answer the questions which an employer chooses to ask has no alternative but to answer, or risk being ruled out of consideration for a job.

What is needed are guidelines restricting the information required to the minimum which is relevant and necessary, together with legal controls ensuring that the information is destroyed as soon as it has served its purpose. Otherwise, the information remains on file — or, as is increasingly likely, on computer — vulnerable to unauthorised access.

Most application forms for the Civil Service are accompanied by information referring, amongst other things, to security requirements. The following paragraph comes from the memorandum given to applicants for schools inspectorships:

> 'All candidates for Civil Service appointments are reminded that the Government have decided that no one may be employed in the Civil Service in connection with work the nature of which is vital to the security of the State if he is or has recently been a member of the British Communist Party or of a Fascist organisation;

> or if in such a way as to raise legitimate doubts about his reliability, he is or has recently been sympathetic to Communism or Fascism, or associated with Communists or Fascists, or their sympathisers, or is susceptible to Communist or Fascist pressure.'

Positive vetting may be carried out before appointment or during early training, or later in a civil servant's career if he or she moves into an area of work which may involve matters of security. The subject of positive vetting has to complete a special questionnaire and submit to background enquiries by 'special investigating officers' from the security services. Not only political sympathies or the wrong kind of friendships may disqualify a candidate; sexual relationships and finances are investigated as well. The last review of public service security procedures was carried out by the Radcliffe Committee which reported in 1962[1]), but no substantial changes were made to the positive vetting system. A civil servant who is transferred or dismissed if positive vetting is unsatisfactory has a right of appeal only to an internal committee of three wise men — known as the Civil Service 'purge tribunal'.

In 1975, NCCL succeeded in having the reference to communist or fascist sympathies deleted from the Training Services Agency's recruitment leaflet for Skillcentre Instructors, since none of the jobs involved security work. But the vague and far-reaching grounds used to decide whether or not someone is safe remain a basis for the kind of witchhunt against so-called extremists which is now being carried out in West Germany.

Teachers

In accordance with regulations made under the Education Act 1944, the Department of Education and Science, together with the Scottish and Welsh Offices, maintain 'List 99', a blacklist of people who may not be employed as teachers or in the youth service. In 1976, the list (of which NCCL was sent a copy anonymously) contained about 1200 names of people either completely banned from teaching, or able to teach only in specified fields of education. A teacher may be banned following a criminal conviction; for 'misconduct' which can include sexual approaches to a pupil or another child or to an adult of the same sex; for conduct 'inappropriate to a teacher' or excessive use of the cane. When Mrs Thatcher was Secretary of State for Education, she warned a teacher who had been convicted of possessing cannabis (outside the school and with no suggestion of pupil involvement) that any similar conduct would lead to an immediate ban. Any procedure which can involve banning teachers on grounds of sexual misconduct has a particularly harsh and discriminatory effect on homosexuals, who find themselves charged with criminal offences for conduct which is entirely legal in heterosexuals (for instance, a consenting homosexual relationship involving someone over the age of 16 but below 21 remains illegal, and homosexual men are often prosecuted for holding hands or kissing in public). Homosexual men are also often persuaded to plead guilty to an offence where they believe themselves to be innocent, for fear of the publicity involved in fighting a case — something that can have disastrous consequences for their future employment.

The Department of Education warns a teacher that a ban is being considered, and the teacher may make written or oral representation. But teachers who have been told they were banned from teaching have not always realised that their names are placed on List 99 and circulated to headteachers and teacher training colleges. In 1976, the Department announced that banned teachers will be specifically informed of their inclusion on the list.

Blacklists and pre-employment checks

In May 1977, workers at Reinforcement Steel Services, a British Steel Corporation subsidiary, found evidence that secret files were being kept on employees with information on their political activities. The workers, who had occupied the factory after the dismissal of some of their colleagues, found a confidential report by the works manager concerning investigations of alleged sabotage. A note from the firm's divisional headquarters said: 'We are advised to keep meticulous records of anything that happens concerning some individuals so as to build up a dossier'. Although the document stated that no proof existed against any of the employees at that plant, two suspects, both active trades unionists, were named. One of them, the report noted, had been checked with the Economic League, who had no record of him on their files. He was said to be an active member of the 'Nationalist Socialist Front movement' (sic), presumably a reference to the Socialist Workers Party, of which he was a member.

The same document showed that during police investigations of the sabotage — which was never proved to have happened — the police had told the works manager that the Special Branch had a file on one of 'the two most likely persons responsible' for his political activities, and that four complaints were on file against him, although details of only three, including 'distributing National Socialist literature', were given. The policeman also told the manager that the other suspect has been bound over for breaking and entering in 1954, when he was 17 — although criminal records are confidential and this particular record would, in any case, be 'spent' under the Rehabilitation of Offenders Act.[2]

The Economic League is a private organisation funded by industry which keeps a blacklist of 'extremists' for use by employers who also contribute much of the information held. It is impossible for a worker to know for certain if he or she is the subject of such a file, or whether an employer is going to refuse him a job for trade union activity, 'militancy', communist associations, homosexuality or some other target of the employer's prejudice. Needless to say, the worker has no legal right whatsoever to see the file or challenge its contents.

Although it is unlawful under the Employment Protection Act 1975 for an employer to dismiss a worker for trade union activity, there is no protection for the worker who is refused a job as a result of being blacklisted. In April 1977, the Employment Appeals Tribunal heard the case of a trade union activist who, knowing that no large employer would take him on because of his record of activity organising building workers into the union, gave a false name and reference to Birmingham Corporation.[3] He was almost immediately recognised and summarily dismissed. The following year, he was taken on by the Corporation at a different site and he was again sacked, on the ground that, the previous year, he had deceived the employer. Although the industrial tribunal upheld his complaint against unfair dismissal, saying that he was protected against victimisation for taking part in trade union activity, the Appeals Tribunal overturned the decision on the ground that, not having been employed for 6 months, he was not covered by the law. The Tribunal recommended that he 'swallow his pride and apologise and ask the Corporation to give him another chance'. The decision revealed that there was no question of the man's having broken the law; he was described by the Appeals Tribunal as having had 'an interesting and stormy career'. In other words, he was an active trades unionist lawfully trying to organise other workers.

As in the public sector, private employers accumulate detailed information on their employees and prospective workers. An application form used by the KGM Group of Companies included questions about parents' nationality, whether the applicant had been convicted of a criminal offence, and whether the applicant was 'in any way' connected with the Communist Party. It included a declaration authorising the company to carry out an investigation to verify the answers to these questions.

Pre-employment checks are increasingly common. But there are severe doubts about the accuracy of the information collected, its relevance to the employment involved, the means used to obtain it, and the use to which it is put. Mr D approached NCCL in 1976 after being refused a job with a security firm. He had been turned down after, he said, a thorough check had been made on his life since he left school. Not only did he not know the reason for the refusal, but it was not until NCCL approached the firm that Mr D received an assurance that the file containing the results of the investigation had been destroyed. Another applicant for a job with a security firm was also turned down after a pre-employment check to which he had agreed. He believed there was nothing in his record to justify refusing him the job, but that 'in a file, somewhere, there is a black mark against me which will permanently damage my prospects.'

Pre-employment checks were discussed in an article in *Top Security,* a trade magazine for private investigators and security firms, which advised, for potential middle and senior managers: 'a background check on their place of residence; their marital status; their outside hobbies and interests; how they get on with their neighbours . . . With extremely senior appointments, we check on the applicants' private habits; his clubs; his interests; and so on'.

The article was also illuminating about the methods of inquiry. 'But we rarely ask questions direct. Instead, we prefer to merge into the background and gain as much information as we can without, obviously, revealing our interest.' In some cases, the article states, the employer asks the applicant to sign an authorisation form which 'in effect, authorises any persons, schools or companies supplying information about him to do so in complete immunity'.

If you apply for a job with a firm which uses pre-employment checks, you are placed in a situation where you can only get a job by agreeing to an open-ended, uncontrolled investigation of your private life. Refusal to authorise the check — if, indeed, authorisation is ever requested — immediately makes you suspect. Whether or not you are them employed depends on the results of an investigation by private operators, who are not licensed or supervised; whose methods are vitually uncontrolled by the criminal law; who may gather gossip and hearsay and grudges and present them as fact; and who are charged with collecting information whose relevance to employment is highly dubious. The report on which the applicant is judged is almost never shown to the applicant, who has no opportunity to challenge its accuracy or relevance and no right to appeal against the decision based on its contents. To make matters worse, there is nothing to prevent the investigator or the employer from passing the report on to a body such as the Economic League, thus ensuring that the injustice suffered once is repeated over and over again.

The applicant who objects to a pre-employment check does not necessarily have 'something to hide'. The applicant may be a homosexual with good grounds for fearing that homosexuality alone will be a reason for refusing employment. NCCL has dealt with a number of cases where individuals have been sacked or victimised because of their homosexuality. The applicant may have a record of trade union activity — fully protected by law — which would disqualify him in the eyes of an employer who refuses to let his workers become unionised. Or you may simply object to having investigators picking over the details of your private life.

References

Like black-lists, references can make it impossible for a person to obtain another job. But you have no effective redress against references which are inaccurate, or even libellous.

> Mr B, an experienced bus-driver, found it impossible to get employment after being made redundant by his firm, although he claimed that his record was accident-free. He had been assured of good references, but was turned down without reason by the first two companies to whom he applied. He obtained a job from a third, but was dismissed shortly afterwards, when references were taken up and obtained by telephone.
> Mr I had been employed as a security guard for 2½ years. He resigned because, he claimed, he was dissatisfied with the staff he worked with and the extent of petty theft in the firm. He was assured by the personnel manager that he would be given a

good reference. Two months after starting employment with
another firm, he was dismissed without notice on the grounds
that his vetting was inadequate. By persuading a friend who ran
a building company to write to his previous employers, he
obtained a copy of the reference they were supplying to
prospective employees, accusing him of misconduct and
incompetence. Mr I consulted solicitors, who were told by the
firm's lawyers that Mr I had 'failed to carry out his duties
properly as a security guard . . . These circumstances would
have justified our clients' dismissing him. However, when your
client's attention was drawn to his unsatisfactory behaviour, he
chose to resign'. In the absence of a hearing for unfair dismissal
— and with no independent body to adjudicate on complaints
about inaccurate records — it is impossible to judge the firm's
claim. But the allegations against Mr I were, he says, never
put to him when he worked with the firm, and he is now
effectively barred from any future job as a security guard. His
solicitor advised an action for libel, but no legal aid is available
and Mr I could not afford the £100 which the solicitor wanted
to start the action.

An ex-student, looking for a first job, is particularly dependent on
references supplied by the college or school. Mr A was the victim of a reference
which was inaccurate and unfair.

Mr A tried for nearly 100 jobs after leaving college in 1976.
Although he had a number of interviews, he was never appointed.
Finally, he obtained a job as a laboratory technician. After he
started work, his employer received references from his former
Head of Department and his college tutor. The Head of Department's
reference said that Mr A had been 'depressed', 'solitary and
withdrawn' and that 'you could not expect much initiative from
him'. In a phone conversation, the Head of Department apparently
told the employer that Mr A had seen his doctor, but that this
had never interfered with his work. Mr A then received a
contract, which said that during his probation period, he would
be subject to medical and other checks to make sure he was
capable of doing the job.
Mr A went to see his Head of Department, who admitted he had
used an 'unfortunate' choice of words, and wrote a second
letter confirming that Mr A had never been treated for depression.
But he refused to withdraw his comments about Mr A's 'withdrawn'
nature or his lack of initiative. Mr A's former tutor, whom he had
seen little of at college, had discussed his own reference with
the Head of Department and also promised Mr A he would write
a letter withdrawing comments in his reference about Mr A's
'depression'. Mr A is now trying to find out how many other
prospective employers were put off by this unexpected and

inaccurate reference to his mental health.

Employers' references may also be given to insurance companies, when the employee needs a 'fidelity guarantee' — i.e. an insurance policy against possible dishonesty.

> Ms F was offered a job by a large firm of retailers, on condition that she was accepted by an insurance company for a £1,000 fidelity guarantee bond. The insurance company, having made enquiries about Ms F's employment record, refused to issue the bond — and Ms F lost her job. Ms F was badly shocked by the refusal, since she knows of nothing in her employment record which would cast doubt on her integrity or honesty. Her MP took the matter up with the Department of Trade, who decided they could not help and that employers' references must remain confidential. Because of secret allegations against her, which she has no chance of challenging or even discovering, Ms F now has no hope of obtaining the employment she wants.

Some employers invite generalised, unsubstantiated and intrusive comments on a prospective employee. NCCL was sent a copy of a form sent by Group 4 Total Security Ltd to another firm, asking for information about a past employee. In addition to factual information about the length of the employment, the form asks for details of why the employee left the company (on which, at least, Group 4 are likely to have heard the employee's own views), and also asks the former employer whether they are aware of 'anything to his/her detriment concerning his/her conduct, work, health, character, integrity, sobriety or financial affairs while employed or in his/her private life?'

The problem of references is very rarely considered in the context of privacy controls. But the refusal of a job on the basis of unverified information which the individual cannot see or challenge is a fundamental denial of the individual's rights. An action for libel is the only remedy which the ex-employee may have. But first of all, he or she has to see a copy of the reference — something which may only be possible by deception. Since qualified privilege attaches to references, the applicant will have to prove that the previous employer was malicious in giving a bad reference. In any case, since legal aid is not available, the remedy is in practice useless for most people.

Colleges and employers usually insist on keeping references secret from former workers or students, often on the grounds that open references would inhibit the referee from being completely frank. Open references might, of course, also inhibit employers or teachers from indulging in criticisms or allegations which had not been put to the individual openly, and which could not be substantiated. It would be much better if the referee felt obliged to warn the individual of anything to his or her detriment which would go into a reference, and to discuss the criticisms of the individual's work. Although employers sometimes threaten to resort to the telephone if written references became open, it would in practice be impossible to make phone enquiries on every occasion. In any case, the individual should at least be able to see and challenge the written record.

Personnel records

Trade unions are increasingly concerned about the extent of personal files kept about employees without their knowledge. Such files may contain information or opinions about an employee's conduct; performance appraisal; information about personal problems; and information or, more probably, reports or opinions about the employee's personal interests, life-style, sexual habits, political views and trade union activities. Such records are used in decisions about transfer, training or promotion; they may be used as the basis for victimisation of an individual; and they will provide a basis for written references in the future. Records which go beyond matters directly related to the job not only invade the individual's right to keep private matters private; they also infringe the right to take part in lawful political or trade union activity, by threatening those whose activities are objectionable to the employer with victimisation at work.

Some unions have made access to personnel records an issue in negotiations. For instance, one NUJ branch has succeeded in winning the right for employees to see their personnel files. The Police Federation has pressed for files on police officers to be open for the individual officer's inspection, although a working party of the Police Advisory Board was only prepared to suggest that reports should be in two parts — one, concerned with job performance, being open for inspection; the other, concerned with recommendations for promotion etc, remaining closed. But most employees have found it impossible to gain access to their records. A teacher who contacted NCCL complained about secret LEA files. His colleague had managed to see the file which apparently contained untrue information, but the teacher could not demand a correction without revealing who had shown him the file. Similarly, NALGO workers in the health service have been disturbed by secret performance reports which can be used as the basis for adverse decisions on an individual from whom the report is kept secret.

A recent International Labour Office study on data-handling and workers' rights suggests that workers should be able to see their files in order to 'correct mistakes, eliminate out-of-date or erroneous information relating to their private life, trade union activity and political leanings or other things that could compromise their careers.' International standards and enforcement machinery should be devised to back up national measures.[4]

In the largest firms or public sector organisations, personnel records may be computerised. In 1975, the National Computer Index showed a total of 812 computer systems which included personnel records, with a further 2,758 computers holding details of wages, salaries and pensions. Computerised records will come under the control of the Data Protection Authority, but the Government's White Paper, instead of proposing a statutory right for the employee to see and challenge such records, suggests that employers may be entitled to withhold some information on 'management grounds'.

(1) Cmnd 1681, HMSO, April 1962
(2) *Guardian,* 23 May 1977
(3) City of Birmingham District Council *v* P L Beyer EAT 560/76
(4) *Computing,* Vol 5 no 24, 16 June 1977

The police and the security services

By 1979, it is estimated that the Police National Computer will hold some 36 million entries — the equivalent of one for nearly each adult member of the community.[1] By the mid 1980's, the Scotland Yard computer alone could be storing information equivalent to one-fifth of the population in the area covered by the Metropolitan Police.[2] The British police have available to them the most sophisticated technology of any police force in the world, but the secrecy surrounding its use has made informed public debate of the implications virtually impossible.

Each of the police forces in the United Kingdom maintains its own information and intelligence records, which are increasingly likely to be computerised. Tayside police force, for instance, has an on-line criminal records system, making it possible to get information about suspects and criminal records at visual display units in the divisional headquarters.[3] Scotland Yard in 1976 announced that an un-named company had been awarded the contract for a massive new computerized system. In addition to the records held by Scotland Yard or by regional forces, the Police National Computer at Hendon maintains information for the use of forces throughout the country.

Police National Computer

The Police National Computer maintains the following information: details of all vehicle owners; disqualified drivers; stolen vehicles; wanted and missing persons; people convicted of criminal records; fingerprints of convicted people; and people subject to a suspended sentence. (The list is taken from the Home Office White Paper[4]); as will be explained below, it is not a strictly accurate description of all the information apparently placed on the computer index.)

The Vehicle Licensing Centre at Swansea, which is run by the Department of the Environment, automatically transfers details of every licensed vehicle to the Police Computer, thus providing the largest single police index of individuals — estimated to amount, by 1979, to 26 million people. In addition to the name, address and date of birth of the owner, and identifying details of the vehicle, the index provides space for further notations — including codes which would alert a police officer enquiring about a vehicle that it was 'temporarily suspected of being used in a crime' or 'of long-term interest to the police'.[5]

Everyone who owns a vehicle must apply to Swansea for registration. But the individual is not told — and the registration application form does not state — that the information will automatically be transferred to the police computer, nor the purpose of the transfer. Despite the Government's assurance that information given for one purpose should not be used for another without either the individual's consent or some other 'authorised justification',6) once again, information provided by an individual for one administrative purpose is transferred, without the individual's consent, to a date bank used in this case for the much more sensitive purpose of crime control and, possibly, political surveillance.

Criminal records, which are held nationally by Scotland Yard as well as by the regional criminal record offices and local forces, have also been computerised. Despite repeated assurances that 'great care is taken to prevent unauthorised disclosure to persons outside the police force', criminal records are notoriously easy to obtain. In September 1976, the *Times* reported that anyone who has obtained the ex-directory phone number of the Criminal Records Office at Scotland Yard (the *Times* obtained it from an informer with a criminal record himself) can, by posing as a police officer, obtain information about an individual's records.7) It is also a boast amongst various private detective and inquiry agencies that they can obtain criminal records, often by employing ex-policemen whose personal links and familiarity with police procedure make it easy to get round security measures.

The police are also required to pass on information about criminal convictions to the relevant professional or public body for any of the following groups of workers: doctors, dentists, nurses, people employed in the care of children, youth leaders, civil servants, atomic energy workers, Post Office employees (temporary and permanent), magistrates, JPs, barristers, solicitors and their clerks. In addition, civil servants must themselves notify their employers of any criminal conviction apart from trivial motoring offences – a practice which the Society of Civil and Public Servants has unsuccessfully tried to change. In 1972, there was considerable outcry about police transfer of information about criminal convictions, following publication of a letter from the Chief Constable in Yorkshire to the Central Midwives' Board concerning a midwife who was dismissed following a theft of drugs. The midwife was not charged with the offence, and the Chief Constable commented in his letter that 'it is known that she has a tumour on her spine; that she has some domestic troubles; and that she has an inferiority complex.' Procedures for passing on information from police records were reviewed following this disclosure, and a new circular (Home Office 140/1973) was issued to police forces.

Later in 1973, after the new circular was produced, NCCL obtained evidence that Air France at Heathrow was clearing new employees through the Criminal Records Office (to which it did not have authorised access) by submitting special forms to the British Airports Authority Police which does have access. Other cases brought to NCCL show that employers have little difficulty in obtaining information. Bristol NCCL reported the case of a woman employed by a supermarket, who was confronted by the store manager a few weeks after starting work and told that he 'knew all about her'. She had one criminal conviction for a minor offence in her teens. The case of Mr T (see page 2) illustrates the consequences to those whose records are disclosed.

In addition to providing information about previous convictions for the occupants of jobs covered by the Home Office circular mentioned above, the police also provide information about prospective foster parents and adopters to the local Social Services Department. The Government notes in its White Paper[8] that this practice 'does not have specific statutory authority'. In other words, it involves a breach of confidence — however well-intentioned — and if the practice is to continue, it should be placed on a proper legal footing. Again apparently without statutory authority, the police provide information to the Criminal Injuries Compensation Board and the Gaming Board.

The Police National Computer also maintains a national fingerprint index. Although described in the White Paper as including prints of convicted people only, Mr Roy Jenkins, when Home Secretary, stated that the fingerprints covered not only people tried and convicted over a 40 year period, but also those awaiting trial.[9] These covered nearly 2½ million people. Furthermore, over 1,500 sets of prints were held in August 1975 of people who had been detained under the Prevention of Terrorism Act. This second number will now be closer to 2½ thousand, since everyone detained under the Act is automatically photographed and fingerprinted. The disturbing point is that, although 95% of those detained under the Act are never charged with a criminal offence, their fingerprints and photographs are to remain on record until the Act is repealed. (Previous 'temporary' legislation lasted 15 years.) Thus, the national fingerprint index has already been extended to include innocent people.

Apart from the Prevention of Terrorism Act, which gives the police the power to force suspects to provide fingerprints, someone arrested by the police does not have to give his or her fingerprints unless the court orders him or her to do so. Where the police take fingerprints following a court order, they are under a legal duty to destroy the prints if the person is later acquitted by the court. But where someone gives prints without a court order being obtained, there is no duty on the police to destroy them although the defendant can apply to the court to have them destroyed. During the picket at Grunwicks in 1976 and 1977, for instance, workers at Brent Law Centre reported that all those arrested had been persuaded to give fingerprints 'voluntarily' because it was made clear that they would be refused bail otherwise. Of the nine people arrested and tried before July 1977, eight were acquitted; can they be sure that, despite the acquittal, the record of their arrest, their name and address, photograph and fingerprints are not now centrally filed?

Consideration should also be given to the length of time for which someone's fingerprints or conviction details should remain on file, where no further offence is committed. It makes nonsense of the Rehabilitation of Offenders Act, for instance, if the fingerprints of someone who committed an offence 40 years ago — a conviction which may now be spent under the Act — remain in a central data-bank, susceptible to unauthorised access.

So far we have discussed records relating mainly to people with a criminal record, but increasingly the police are collecting and storing information, not on people with a record, but on suspects and 'known associates', with the aim of maintaining detailed profiles of people who may commit a crime in future, although they have not done so yet. The Criminal Intelligence Unit (C11) of Scotland Yard, together with the regional crime squads, collates information from informers and from surveillance, including extensive details of the friends and personal lives of their suspects. Whereas an arrest should be based on reasonable suspicion that the suspect has committed a criminal offence, the surveillance involved in information-gathering starts several stages before reasonable suspicion can exist — so that someone innocent of criminal involvement, or against whom no evidence exists, may become the target of special enquiries, phone-tapping or mail interception as a result of mixing with the 'wrong' people. The Thames Valley police are participating in an experiment using a computer to collate an enormous quantity of apparently insignificant and unrelated information, as part of this process of 'pre-emptive policing'. While the police have always sought to anticipate crime, particularly by maintaining close links with criminals and informers, the technology now at their disposal — and the absence of effective legal controls over police investigations — makes it possible for the police to invade someone's privacy on a massive scale, entirely reversing the assumption of innocence until guilt is proved.

Of the 52 police forces in the United Kingdom, Scotland Yard is responsible for the largest information gathering exercises. In 1977, the *Times*[10] carried a report on the Yard's proposed new computerised system, which will provide a highly sophisticated information retrieval service for branches of the Metropolitan Police. According to the White Paper[11], this data bank will hold information about 'crime, criminals and their associates'. For instance, by 1985 the computer will hold details on about 72,000 people and 32,000 companies, including details of bankruptcies. In 1974, the equivalent manual files covered 26,500 individuals and 15,500 companies, and the information is presumably collected and used by the fraud squad.

The second area covered by the Scotland Yard computer concerns criminals and organised crime, expected by 1985 to grow to 193,500 records. In 1974, the records covered 130 main criminals, 2,500 'key' criminals and 60,000 others. Presumably this group of records would include those maintained by C 11 (Criminal Intelligence), who are estimated to hold about 8,000 dossiers. It may also include the records collected by the National Drugs Intelligence Unit and the National Immigration Intelligence Unit, which collect and disseminate information not only on known drugs offenders or illegal immigrants, but also on suspects. The largest group of Scotland Yard files, according to the *Times* report, covered 1,150,000 names in 1974. Only about half these files are likely to be computerised.

The *Times* asked Scotland Yard why information about the computer system was considered 'classified' if the records were only criminal records; what categories of records, from which branches of the force, would be computerised; whether one section of the files concerned political, terrorist or 'subversive' activity; whether two-thirds of the largest section of records concerned suspects and associates rather than people with criminal records; and what percentage of the records concerned convicted criminals. Scotland

Yard refused to provide any of the information requested, on the grounds that answers would breach security. Thus the press, MPs and the public are left speculating about the sources of the information to be computerised; the groups and numbers of individuals involved; the criteria for defining someone as a 'suspect', an 'associate' or a 'subversive'; and the use to which the information will be put.

The Scotland Yard records on an unidentified group of just over 1 million people, as well as the records on crime, criminals and their associates, will, presumably, include Special Branch material on suspected terrorists and on political activists. Attempts to obtain information about the budget or staff of the Special Branch, the number of people on whom it holds political files or the criteria used for selecting those people, have got nowhere with Home Office Ministers. In addition to other duties, the Branch maintains surveillance of organisations and individuals who might pose a threat to internal order and is, of course, particularly involved in collecting information on the Irish community in Britain. It has a special responsibility for investigating offences under the Official Secrets Act; it vets applicants for naturalisation and maintains watch at ports and airports, watching for undesirable entrants and logging the movements of political activists[12].

The Special Branch was initially formed as a response to Irish bombings in London. It now maintains extensive and detailed records on Irish people living in Britain and on people involved in political activities relating to Ireland — including, for instance, trade union militants who happen to be Irish; those involved in Republican activity; prisoners' support groups; and organisations challenging Government policy, such as the British Withdrawal from Northern Ireland Campaign or the Troops Out Movement. In 1976, an American woman visiting Britain, who had intended to visit the Anti-Imperialist Festival held annually in Ireland, was refused entry to this country because her name was on the list of Festival visitors held by the Special Branch officer at the airport. The Prevention of Terrorism Act, allowing up to 7 days' detention for questioning without charge, has given the Special Branch new opportunities for gathering information about the political views and activities of Irish people or those concerned with Ireland — even though, as mentioned above, there is no evidence that the vast majority of those arrested are involved in criminal activity.

The Special Branch also maintains information on large numbers of people who are politically active in organisations which the Branch considers subversive — the Stop the Seventy Tour Committee, the Vietnam Solidarity Campaign or the Agee-Hosenball Defence Committee, for instance — as well as members of, on the one hand, the National Front and other extreme right groups and, on the other, the Communist Party, Socialist Workers Party and other left groups, together with at least some leftwing members of the Labour Party.

The low-level intelligence contained in the Special Branch index cards (as distinct from files held on a smaller number of 'key' activists) is mainly obtained from public sources — careful reading of the political press, for example. The Branch indexes the name of those signing petitions. Its officers assiduously collect careless talk from people involved, even if only on the fringes, of political activity, in some cases paying or persuading people to become informers. When someone is arrested (or detained under the anti-terrorist laws), or a house or office raided, address books and mailing lists are confiscated and contents indexed and cross-referenced. Employers are contacted, or volunteer information. In 1977, for instance, the National Union of Teachers in East Sussex contacted NCCL with reports that Special Branch officers had visited headteachers in Eastbourne and Newhaven in search of information on 'political extremists'. The Chief Constable of Sussex Police Force told NCCL that 'It is of course a fact of life that the Police make enquiries from time to time in a whole general area so as to discharge their basic function of maintaining the Queen's peace. No further comment is, therefore, feasible on the query which is raised in your mind as the action of the Police in the area of general enquiries to which I refer has always been necessary and appropriate.' The Sussex police, it seems, regards themselves as free to pry into the beliefs and lawful activities of those they label 'extremists'.

In some cases, the Branch (like the CID and other divisions of the police) steps up its surveillance by getting a warrant for a telephone tap or mail-opening. In 1956, the Birkett Committee announced the figures for warrants for years between 1937 and 1955; in 1955, for instance, 231 phones were tapped and 205 people had their mail intercepted. Since then, no figures have been announced, on the grounds that this information would be too helpful to those under surveillance! The decision to authorise a tap or mail interception rests with the Home Secretary alone. In early 1977, for instance, NCCL was given fairly reliable information that its phone was being tapped as a result of the Agee Hosenball campaign, while the arrest under the Official Secrets Acts of Aubrey, Berry and Campbell (all involved in the same campgain) must have involved the tapping of other phones.

Phone taps are not the only way in which the police obtain information about an individual's telephone calls. The Post Office itself obtains information about the destination of trunk calls which can be made available to the renter of the line (for instance, to an employer wanting to monitor the cost of employees' calls). The information may also be made available to the police — without the customer's knowledge. According to internal Post Office memoranda, requests from the police for information about trunk calls are referred to the Area Traffic Divisions who, according to a letter from the Post Office to NCCL, 'must be satisfied that the information is vital to police enquiries in a matter of serious crime, and cannot be obtained from other sources'. The police and the Post Office between them make the decision which, the Post Office claims, 'does not need express statutory authority'.

Readers who are not themselves involved politically or in a trade union may wonder why the activities of the Special Branch should worry anyone whose own activities are lawful. The first point to make is that the activities of the vast majority of the people on whom the Special Branch maintain files are indeed lawful, and that the Special Branch's operation represents very real interference with the freedom — upheld in democratic theory — to associate with others for any lawful purpose. The monitoring of people's political involvement is an invasion of their privacy which undermines the legitimate expectation that someone's *beliefs* and lawful acts will not be monitored by the state.

In deciding which individuals and which organisations are 'subversive', the Special Branch inevitably comes to regard as the enemy those who disagree with the current political orthodoxy. Thus, in relation to Northern Ireland, those who wish to see troops withdrawn from Northern Ireland are regarded as subversives or likely to aid republican terrorists: one pacifist campaigner against the Army's role in Northern Ireland was arrested under the Prevention of Terrorism Act.[13] Dissident groups — even where their activities are confined to organising meetings, leafletting, selling newspapers, involvement with community or trade union affairs etc — are treated in the same way as target criminals. Trade unionists known for their militant stand are regarded as a threat to state security.

Collecting information is not, of course, the end in itself. Nor is the Special Branch operation simply designed to maintain familiarity with different groups which might, one day in the future, fall under reasonable suspicion of serious criminal offences. The criminal law allows the police wide scope in taking action against individuals or groups they dislike, sometimes without even the need to present a case in front of the courts. The information which formed the basis for the deportations of Philip Agee and Mark Hosenball was collected by DI 5 (MI5) and the Special Branch: it was never presented to the deportees, to be subjected to cross-examination and challenge in the usual way. The recent allegation of a mix-up in MI5 files on Judith Hart MP and Will Owen MP[14] can only add to the suspicions about the reliability of the information presented to Merlyn Rees as Home Secretary. We have already mentioned the case of the American woman refused entry to the UK for a visit because her name was on the list of prospective visitors to the anti-imperialist festival: the immigration officer, advised by the Special Branch, was able to turn her away, even though she had had to cancel her plans to attend the festival and even though the festival itself was a lawful meeting.

The Prevention of Terrorism Act provides a new means of taking executive action against someone, even where the police have no evidence to justify a criminal charge. The Home Secretary has made exclusion orders against 90 people, who have no knowledge of the allegations against them, no opportunity to contest the evidence and no right of appeal to a court. Twenty have made representations to an adviser appointed by the Home Secretary and six have been successful in having the orders revoked. The rest have been excluded from Britain by a procedure which removes every safeguard provided in the system of criminal justice, and which gives dangerous and unacceptable scope for Special Branch activity.

Finally, the use of conspiracy charges have enabled the police to use the information collected about friendship networks and associations as evidence in criminal cases. Normally, evidence which could prejudice a defendant by association — for instance, about his friends or his reading material — is not admitted in a criminal trial. In a conspiracy case, however, evidence that one defendant knew another, evidence of common membership of a group or shared involvement in a campaign — evidence, in other words, of precisely the kind gathered by the Special Branch from address books and membership lists — is admitted and can lead to a conviction even where there is no substantive evidence of involvement in a crime. Although the Criminal Law Act 1976 makes some reforms to the conspiracy laws, particularly as regards sentencing, the question of evidence is left untouched.

If the Special Branch's work is shadowy, the public is kept entirely in the dark about military and defence intelligence — DI5 (formerly MI5), DI6 (MI6) and the Defence Intelligence Staff. DI5, which is responsible for positive vetting of civil servants likely to come into contact with security material, works closely with the Special Branch, who share information with it and may help in the final stages of an investigation, by making arrests, preparing evidence for trial and appearing in court. The Government Communications Headquarters in Cheltenham, amongst other activities, intercepts diplomatic messages and monitors all telegrams and telexes leaving this country. DI5 is in theory responsible to the Home Secretary, but its director has direct access to the Prime Minister. The directive issued by Mr Maxwell-Fyfe when he was Home Secretary in 1952, setting out the relationship between MI5 and the Minister, and published in Lord Denning's report on the Profumo affair, leaves DI5 free to define what activities are 'subversive of the State' and therefore worthy of DI5's attention, and states that the Home Secretary is not to be provided with detailed information, but only with 'such information as may be necessary' — that is to say, only such information as DI5 considers necessary. Sir Harold Wilson, who, as Prime Minister, was ultimately responsible for security, has recently stated that: 'I am not certain that for the last eight months when I was Prime Minister I knew what was happening fully in security.'

The security forces are not established by Act of Parliament. Their existence is not even recognised in the common law. The complete absence of democratic accountability was criticised in a recent article in *International Affairs,* the journal of the Royal Institute for International Affairs. In the United States, in striking contrast to British practice, the operation of intelligence services can be questioned and debated by the Intelligence Oversight Board and the Select Intelligence Committee of the Senate. As a result of the Freedom of Information Act, individuals are able to obtain copies, or in some cases extracts, of files held on them by the CIA and the FBI — a process which has revealed, amongst other things, the extent of phone-tapping of those involved in the anti-war movement. When the security services of the United States of America can be subjected to this degree of public scrutiny, the British insistence on secrecy — the refusal to answer Parliamentary Questions or permit Parliamentary debate; the operation of the Official Secrets Acts; the deportation of two journalists who had published embarrassing material — appears both ludicrous and indefensible.

Terrorist violence in Northern Ireland led the Army to undertake a massive information-gathering exercise, with the aid of computer facilities which could record, for virtually immediate retrieval, detailed information about every home and individual resident in key areas, right down to the colour of the sofa and the curtains in each front room. Information gathered could be used, not as evidence in court proceedings, but as the basis for arrest or internment (it was widely reported, for instance, that six 'traces' against a person — such as being seen in the wrong company — led to an arrest). In the rest of the United Kingdom, the spread of terrorist crime led to the Prevention of Terrorism Act and to extensive surveillance of the Irish community and those involved in Irish politics. The Incitement to Disaffection Act 1934 — unused since before World War II — was revived in prosecutions against pacifists and others who had advised soldiers about the role of the Army in Northern Ireland, until the acquttal of fourteen members of the British Withdrawal from Northern Ireland Campaign in 1975 led to the abandoning of other charges pending under the Act. It is not surprising that any Government or police measure seems acceptable in the drive to stop bombings and assassination. But the effect is to undermine fundamental democratic rights — without helping to solve the conflict from which the violence springs. This country has rejected 'political crime' as a legal or penal category and those convicted of terrorist offences do not get 'political status' in prison. But it institutionalises the notion of political crime in police operations which have as their targets people's political views — however peaceful their activities.

On the one hand, this country's liberal democracy claims to extend freedom of thought and speech and the right to associate even to those who fundamentally disagree with the present organisation of the state, reserving criminal sanctions for those who organise or incite violent opposition. On the other hand, the state takes measures to protect itself against 'subversion', which inevitably involve infringing the rights of those who dissent and which undermine the expectation that people will be allowed to hold their beliefs — however much others disagree — and organise peacefully without state interference. The conflict has been resolved only by ignoring in practice the claims of free speech and expression, by extending the resources of the security services, dramatically increasing the capacity of the police for political surveillance, resorting to extra-judicial means as a way of taking action against 'subversives' and keeping the entire operation, and the real questions it raises about individual privacy and democratic freedom, as secret as possible.

(1) *The Political Police in Britain,* Bunyan, Quartet 1977 (revised edn) p 86
(2) *Times,* 14 February 1977
(3) *Police Review,* 7 January 1977
(4) Cmnd 6354, Table 1
(5) Bunyan, p 86
(6) Cmnd 6353, para 34
(7) *Times,* 11 September 1976
(8) Cmnd 6354, para 41
(9) *Daily Telegraph,* 8 May 1976
(10) *Times,* 14 February 1977
(11) Cmnd 6354, para 45
(12) See Bunyan for the most detailed account available of the Special Branch
(13) The person arrested was Pat Arrowsmith who recovered damages as a result of an action against the police for false imprisonment.
(14) *Observer,* 17 July 1977

Cash, credit and computers

In this section, we take a look at the way credit reference agencies work and a new law, the Consumer Credit Act 1974, which gives people the right to see their own files. We also consider the issue of banks and privacy.

Credit reference agencies

Hundreds of credit reference agencies in the United Kingdom supply information about the credit-worthiness and financial status of individuals. Many of them double as debt-collecting agencies. Some of them, like the United Association for the Protection of Trade, work on a co-operative basis, with retailers exchanging details of bad payers through a central registry. Others like Credit Data (formerly British Debt Services) provide a commercial service. Under the Consumer Credit Act, such agencies must be licensed by the Director General of Fair Trading, although by July 1977 the licensing process was not yet complete. There are no precise figures for the number of individuals covered by these agencies, but the total must be well over 20 million.

Some of these organisations collect information which is publicly available — in particular details of judgments made in the County Court against debtors. A register is kept in London of every judgment for a debt of £10 or more which remains unpaid for a month. In 1976, the Lord Chancellor proposed to abolish the register — which can be inspected on payment of a fee of £1 by post for a 5-year search or 50p for a search in person — on the grounds that it was 'an unnecessary invasion of privacy'. But the proposal was withdrawn after protests from consumer groups and credit reference agencies. The Government has, however, raised the amount of debts to be included on the list to £50 (Administration of Justice Act 1976) and proposes in future to ensure that a person's name will be automatically removed from the register when the debt is paid. At the moment, the name stays on the list unless the individual applies for it to be deleted and pays a fee.

The County Court debtors' register does not necessarily mean that accurate information is supplied to credit reference agencies. A judgment against one person may be listed by the agency against someone else with the same, or a similar, name. Under the present system, someone's name stays on the register long after the debt was paid and does not state, for instance, if the debt was paid off promptly or by regular instalments after the judgment was made. Nor does the register give any information about the background to the debt — for instance, if the person was seriously ill at the time. On page 1, we quoted one example of the damage that can be caused by this kind of mistake. The following complaints are taken from letters received by NCCL.

'In 1970, while single and living with my parents, my mother and father had county court judgments against them. In October 1970, I married and now live in a different town. Recently I applied for hire purchase on a colour TV and got refused. I found out I was on the bad debt society lists and that the judgment against my parents had followed me as my father has the same name as myself . . . . I have tried several times to get my name cleared from the list but have not yet been successful as I cannot get their address.'

'Just recently we applied to the AA of which we are members for a personal loan. They refused us and gave no reason. We then got in touch with N . . . . . Finance Co. from whom we had a previous loan in 1971, which was repaid in full in 6 months. This company wrote back saying they couldn't entertain us as we were too bad a risk. We've since applied to two or three other companies and received the same reply. This we cannot understand as we had never owed money anywhere. In fact, we've had letters in the past saying we were good payers . . . We've no idea why everybody suddenly tells us we are a very bad risk without giving any reason.'

These letters were written before the Consumer Credit Act 1974 came into effect. On page 76, we explain what difference the Act will make.

A number of people also find themselves refused credit because of the record of someone else who once lived at the same address.

'I have reason to believe that my name is on some kind of blacklist. In the past few months I have written to several mail order firms, to run one of their catalogues and have been refused every time. Although I have run a Grattan Catalogue for nearly ten years with no problem. I know of no reason why I should be refused because neither my husband or myself have ever been in debt. The only thing I can think of is when his brother lived with us he may have got into debt, but he no longer is at our address so I don't see why we should suffer for something we haven't done.'

In another case, a woman complained that she had been refused credit on the grounds that her lodger, who had left her house ten years previously, had run up a number of debts. Providing the information about the previous occupant is accurate, there seems to be nothing in the Consumer Credit Act to prevent people being blacklisted because of their address. Similarly, some gas and electricity boards insist on deposits before connection from people living in particular areas, regardless of the credit-worthiness of the individual or family concerned.

In 1975, NCCL was sent a copy of a bad debtors' directory, consisting of names and, in some cases, aliases; addresses or last known address; and the type of goods on which the individual is alleged to have defaulted. The sketchiness of the information makes it inevitable that people with the same surnames will be confused. The directory gives no source for the information, the date on which each debt was allegedly incurred, nor whether there was any dispute over, for instance, the quality of the goods bought. Although the firm compiling the directory appeared to have gone out of business, copies were still in circulation.

In addition to the information obtained from the County Court register or from individual retailers, finance houses accumulate extremely detailed information about people applying for HP or other loans. A couple attempting to buy a musical instrument for their child on hire purchase, paying £50 deposit and borrowing a further £45, were asked to complete a form for an unnamed finance house, giving details of marital status, dependent children, wife's maiden name, length of time at present address, phone number, nature of accommodation (rented or bought), name and address of landlord or mortgagee, employer's name, address and phone number, applicant's occupation and salary bracket, wife's occupation and average weekly income, and the ages of any children under 17 years. All this in addition to details of two existing credit accounts for reference, name and address of bank and the amount on current and deposit accounts, and the name and address of two relatives or friends (not neighbours) who, according to the form, would *not* be approached regarding the application! When this form was brought to the attention of the Office of Fair Trading, the answer was simply that the Consumer Credit Act placed no restrictions on the information which a finance company could demand from someone seeking credit. As a result, detailed information finds its way into the records of finance houses — together with information about creditors' relatives and friends — with no legal restrictions whatsoever to stop the finance house passing on the information to any government official or private agency who asks for it.

The Glasgow *Sunday Mail* reported an instance, at the end of 1975, of the carelessness with which some organisations apparently treat confidential information. A postman sent 25p to British Debt Services in Manchester, asking for a copy of his own credit reference file. He received his own file — together with a document listing £300 worth of bad debts incurred by other people, their names and the dates on which they appeared in court.

Just how inaccurate consumer credit files can be was illustrated in a court case in the United States of America in 1976. TRW Credit Data keeps files on 50 million people and issues 10 million reports a year. It is a firm with a good record for accuracy. Following the introduction of a law which gives people the right to see their credit reference files in the United States, about 2 per cent, or 200,000 of these files were challenged by the individuals concerned. TRW admitted that, as a result, it changed one-third of those files. Thus, over 70,000 files in the world's largest private computer data bank were wrong and had to be changed.[1])

In addition to the fairly limited information on an individual's credit-worthiness provided by commercial credit reference agencies, many also provide 'status reports' — detailed accounts of an individual's financial position, which may be compiled from conversations with neighbours, tradespeople and other contacts, as well as from more orthodox sources. A status report seen by NCCL had as its subject a Member of Parliament.

The information in the report included an alleged purchase, in his secretary's name, of a flat in London, speculation about his sexual relationship with the secretary, and comments, supposedly from his local party agent, that he had no other source of income than his MP's salary and occasional earnings from writings and that he had an overdraft at the bank.

Such a report was based on gossip and hearsay. The methods of some credit reference agencies go beyond the unpleasant to the unlawful. In 1969, the directors of Tracing Services Ltd (the firm responsible for the MP's status report) were convicted of conspiring to effect a public mischief by employing agents to pose as tax inspectors, DHSS officials and policemen in order to obtain confidential information. TSL went into liquidation in 1974, although a number of its subsidiaries remain in operation. The directors convicted in 1969 are no longer involved with the firm.

Were TSL to resurrect themselves in 1977, using the methods for which they were convicted, it is unlikely that they could even be prosecuted. In 1974, in the case of *Withers,* the House of Lords decided that the offence for which the TSL directors were convicted − 'conspiring to effect a public mischief' − does not exist.[2] The House of Lords' decision is particularly important, since it involved two private investigators, the Withers brothers, who had used bugging devices in a hotal bedroom to get evidence for a divorce case. Convicted of conspiracy to effect a public mischief, they appealed and the conviction was eventually quashed. There is now a serious gap in the law, which means that the most objectionable methods used by some credit reference agencies and private detectives are no longer criminal offences.[3]

The public sale of collections of credit reference files poses a new threat to individual privacy. When TSL went into liquidation in 1974 (so much for its earlier gradiose plans to computerise files on the entire population), its 5 million files were acquired, along with other assets, by a company dealing with credit checks on businesses. The files lay unused in warehouses in London and Manchester, until they were advertised for sale to the highest bidder in January 1975. Their value, it was claimed, was £5,000. As a result of the protests against their sale, the files were sold to NCCL for 1p and destroyed, although the Manchester files had been in the process of being sold to a Scottish credit reference agency.

Only a month after the destruction of the TSL files, a Northern firm, North East Debt and Commercial Services, went into liquidation and it was announced that their three million files would be offered on the open market. Despite protests to the creditors and a local newspaper campaign against the sale, the Official Receiver proceeded to put the files up for sale − although in fact he failed to find a buyer. Similarly, when the Department of Trade and Industry was involved in the liquidation of Vehicle and General Insurance Company, they saw nothing wrong in the sale of hundreds of thousands of its private files.

Finally, it is a common tactic of agencies which combine debt-collecting with providing credit references to harass people by threatening to place them on national bad debtors' lists. A typical letter comes from Manaton Central Register of Defaulters Ltd:

> 'Dear Sir/Madam
>
> 'We have been advised by the above that despite applications by them you have defaulted in payment of your account.
>
> 'Therefore please take notice that failure by you to make payment direct to this creditor within the next seven days may result in your name being registered as a defaulter both locally and nationally. This registration could stop you obtaining any further credit in future.'

In this case, the account had been settled when it was only one month overdue.

In another case, two sisters received a letter from Professional and Trade Services Limited of London, demanding payment of £2.36 which it was alleged the sisters owed to a local newsagents, together with a recovery fee of 60p. The letter threatened legal proceedings if payment was not made. The women had closed their account with the newsagents a year previously and, after a few months, destroyed the receipts; but they confirmed that the newsagents' books showed that the account had been closed. They had received no demand for further payment from the firm. Although they demanded from Professional and Trade Services information about the goods on which the debt had allegedly been incurred, and the date of the debt, nothing further was heard. The women, who objected strongly to what they described as 'virtually a demand for money with menace', are now scared that their names have been placed on a debtors' black list.

The Administration of Justice Act 1970 makes harassment of debtors a criminal offence. It seems to have had little effect on the practices of some of these agencies. Only 24 prosecutions were brought between 1970 and the end of 1975, and 17 people were convicted and fined.

The Consumer Credit Act 1974

The Consumer Credit Act completely rewrites the law governing relations between the individual consumer and the retailer or finance company.
It makes two main changes which affect credit references agencies. Firstly, these agencies must now be licensed by the Director General of Fair Trading, who has powers to refuse a licence where he is not satisfied with the conduct of an agency or the people proposing to set one up. One effect of the licensing procedure will be that files put on the market by companies such as North East Debt and Commercial Services can only be sold to licensed agencies or an agency able to obtain a licence. It is, however, too early to say whether the licensing system will effectively control, or put out of business, those on the shadier end of the credit reference business.

Secondly, the Act now gives individuals the right to see and challenge a file kept by a credit reference agency. (A full guide to your rights is available in a separate NCCL leaflet.) This part of the Act came into effect in May 1977. Someone applying for credit will also be able to find out what credit reference agency, if any, will be approached for a report. The consumer can then demand from the agency, in return for 25p, a full copy in plain English of any information they have. If the information is wrong, the consumer can insist that the agency correct it and can also add a note of

up to 200 words giving his or her side of the story. The Director General of Fair Trading has the power to deal with complaints from a consumer about a credit reference file and can order the agency to amend the file. These new rights will give the individual consumer more control over credit reference files than any other kind of information system. But the Act still does not deal with all the problems posed by credit reference systems.

Firstly, the Act does not affect the *methods* used by credit reference agencies, whose investigators can continue to gossip to neighbours or try and delve into criminal records or tax files in order to get information for their files. It will be little comfort to be able to correct information from a tax form or a social security file which has found its way into your credit reference file, if this information should never have got there in the first place.

Secondly, there is nothing to stop agencies collecting irrelevant information. As the American Civil Liberties Union commented on the equivalent United States law — the Fair Credit Reporting Act — 'There is nothing to prevent an investigative agency from poking around the neighbourhood inquiring into your politics, your sex life, your marital problems, your drinking habits or from reporting what it finds to your prospective employer or insurer'.[4] The Office of Fair Trading should draw up a Code of Practice for the standards of relevance which should be met by credit reference agencies, and refuse an operating licence to agencies which do not comply. In particular, it should not be possible to blacklist an individual for a debt incurred by someone else at the same address.

Thirdly, there is no limit on the time during which credit reference agencies can keep information. A debt judgment can stay on the record for years:

> 'I myself have had the unfortunate situation whereby I was put into court for two debts and not large amounts at that, I paid these off in 1970. Since then my chances of credit have been nil with finance companies. On Saturday (in 1976) my youngest son went to a shop to put a deposit on a moped and I had to ask my elder son to be guarantor. Now today I get a phone call from the shop. The finance company want to know why my husband wouldn't be guarantor; being honest, I told him and I now have to tell my youngest son that he can't have a bike because years ago we had been to court.'

Fourthly, the Consumer Credit Act does not require agencies to pass on the correction made by a consumer to any firms which have received the information within, say, the previous six months. The United States Fair Credit Reporting Act places a duty on agencies to circulate a correction and a similar provision is needed here.

The Act also contains a number of exemptions. The consumer can only obtain the information about the name of the credit reference agency involved if the application for credit involves a sum of less than £5,000. Although private mortgages are covered, local authority and building society mortgages are exempt. Furthermore, the individual has no right to see a reference obtained by a bank, nor can the consumer do anything about the contents of a file kept by the retailer's own credit control section. Many large department stores, for instance, use their own files, rather than a credit reference agency but the individual has no right to see or correct the store's own files.

It is also unfortunate that the Act places the onus on the individual consumer to find out which agency is being applied to for a report — rather than making disclosure of such information automatic when credit is applied for — and to obtain a copy of the file. The American Civil Liberties Union argues that credit reference agencies should be required to inform every individual on whom they have a file or plan to open one. 'If it costs the credit industry more and that cost must be passed on to all of us, so be it. In so far as the amount of that cost is concerned, it is suggested that it cannot be more than pennies per person and that the known damage done to untold millions which can and will be corrected when people learn of their rights is a benefit to society far outweighing the cost to the industry.[5]) At least one American study of computerised files suggests that if enough people apply to see their file, it becomes cheaper to send a copy of the file to everyone.

Finally, the Consumer Credit Act still leaves the individual with little redress against an agency which has distributed damaging information. An organisation which maliciously distributes information knowing it to be inaccurate or unreliable could, in theory, be sued for libel. But a libel action has to be brought in the High Court; no legal aid is available and very few people are likely to risk a long, complex and expensive court case. In order to protect people from libellous information, it is necessary to change the law to provide legal aid in libel cases and to ensure that such cases can be brought in the County Court.

Computerisation

Most credit reference agencies in this country keep their records manually. The TSL records, bought by NCCL in 1975, were simply cards in index filing cabinets, containing brief information about the applicant, proposed guarantor, the item for which credit was required and whether or not credit should be given. In 1970, British Debt Services bought the electoral register for the entire country, as the basis for a comprehensive system; although they have a computer facility for their other operations, they have not computerised their individual credit references.

According to the National Computer Index, 1,342 computers kept credit control information on individuals in June 1975. Of these, 224 were in insurance, banking, finance and business, while the next largest single group, 163, were in the distributive trades. Credit reference — as distinct from credit control (internal records maintained by a department store or public facility) —account for only a small proportion of computerised credit data.

The Consumer Credit Act does not give consumers the right to see or challange files held in the credit control section of a retail firm or nationalised industry. But computerised records will come under the control of the proposed Data Protection Authority, which the Government is committed to set up (see page 89 for more information on the proposed Authority). There will therefore, be two overlapping bodies and laws covering credit information: the Consumer Credit Act and Director General of Fair Trading covering credit reference files, whether computerised or not; and the Data Protection Act and Authority covering computerised data banks, including both credit reference and credit control records. NCCL has proposed that there should be a single Authority covering computerised and manual data banks.

We have already described the dangers to individual privacy involved in irrelevant, inaccurate, out of date or unlawfully obtained information. Computerisation makes it possible to store more information, on more and more people, until every adult in the country is filed in computerised credit reference and control banks. The computer also makes virtually instant recall of the information possible: a remote terminal allows the operator to obtain, within seconds, a full print-out from the central computer on the person applying for credit. Unless rigorous safeguards, backed by law, are built into the system, there is a serious danger that someone with no right to see an individual's file will gain access to it, by 'tapping' the computer centrally or via a terminal; by making an enquiry under the pretence of being a finance house or retailer; or by persuading or bribing an employee of the agency to pass on the information.

Unfortunately, the right of individuals to request a correction to their file can itself provide an opportunity for new frauds. In 1976, a Federal Grand Jury in Los Angeles charged six people with altering the records of TRW Credit Data, the credit reference firm referred to earlier. A clerk in the consumer relations department, which makes some 70,000 corrections each year to the records held on 50 million people, allegedly changed over 100 records which were in fact accurate, deleting references to slow or non-payment and, in some cases, inserting details of fictitious loans which had been apparently paid off promptly. The changes allegedly led to frauds of at least $1 million.[6] This case, involving a company with 2,500 remote terminals in 100 cities, illustrates the need for tough security precautions inside credit reference agencies.

Safeguards raise the question of cost. One estimate from United States researchers[7] suggests that the annual cost of converting a computerised credit reference system covering 35 million individuals to comply with privacy safeguards could be 146% of the previous annual operating cost. The same researchers suggest that the cost of sending a copy of his record to every person each year would average 20 cents, compared with a cost of $1.40 for notifying each person who requests a copy: if more than 14% of the people covered by the system apply for a copy of their file in one year, it becomes cheaper to send everyone a copy. But these estimates are highly speculative: estimates of the additional cost of safeguards for different systems vary from 11% to 146% in this study alone, while it is reported that in West Germany an additional possible cost of only 1% has been suggested as realistic. It is interesting to note that, under the Consumer Credit Act, the individual wanting to see a copy of his or her file will have to pay 25p which was at the time the Act went through about the usual charge to a retailer wanting to check up on a customer.

Safeguards

Information in a credit reference or control file can range from the name and address of the consumer, name and address of a guarantor and a note about whether any complaints have been made about the consumer, to a complete profile of the individual — including name and address of spouse, reference to family, neighbours and friends, details of job, income, housing, hire purchase, loans, credit card purchases and standing in the neighbourhood. People who might be interested in acquiring an individual's record include journalists, tax inspectors, social security officials, local government, employers, malicious neighbours, the police and the security services. At the moment, there is nothing to stop them doing so.

The following safeguards must be incorporated in a new privacy law:
— People applying for credit should be asked to give permission for application to be made to a credit reference agency.
— The limited protection given by the Consumer Credit Act should be extended to credit control records held by the retail firm itself.
— There should be a positive duty on agencies holding data banks to inform each subject and to supply a copy of the file annually.
— Any correction made to the individual's file should be forwarded to those who have received the file within the previous six months.
— The Director General for Fair Trading or the new Data Protection Authority should draw up guidelines, to be given statutory backing, for the standards of relevance which should apply to information gathered for credit reference or control records, and the time-limits which should apply to the storing of the information.
— It should be a criminal offence for a credit agency to obtain confidential information by deception, and the individual should be able to sue for damages for misuse of information unlawfully obtained.
— It should be unlawful for anyone other than an organisation authorised by the individual concerned to obtain a copy of the individual's record.

Given the new right of individuals to see their own files, an unauthorised investigator may in future pretend to be the person whose file he wants to see and forge that person's signature. Similarly, unless safeguards are introduced to limit enquiries to those authorised by the individual, the investigator may claim to be a retailer enquiring about a new customer. This kind of deception should be covered by the criminal law, but the only way of detecting it may be to provide each individual with an 'information statement', like a bank statement listing the people to whom information has been given and on what dates.

Banks

Although banks place great stress on the confidentiality of the records they maintain, it is normal practice for them to provide confidential references (although not details of transactions) to other banking institutions, including credit-card companies. As the Younger Committee commented[8], this practice is not as well-known and accepted amongst customers as the banks claim and it is hard to believe that an individual opening an account realises that he or she is supposed to be giving consent to this practice.

In 1971, the *Guardian* provided disturbing evidence of the inadequate security arrangements of at least two banks. Within 48 hours and using the telephone only, reporters obtained a full dossier on the news editor, including information from two banks about the balance in hand, the amount of her monthly salary and the name of her husband. Although the banks, in evidence to the Younger Committee, found it hard to believe that this could happen, the fact was that it had happened and revealed an unfortunate gap in the banks' security arrangements. Bank customers who obtain details of their bank balance by phoning and giving an account number should realise that someone else, having obtained the account number, could also obtain the financial information.

The cashless society?

Computerisation in banking and finance has made it possible to foresee a time when people will do without cash or cheques entirely. Although the cashless society is not going to arrive for some time, even in the United States, experiments are being carried out there and, in this country, research is being undertaken under the auspices of the Inter-Bank Research Organisation.

The cashless society would combine credit cards with computerised bank records and credit reference files. Remote terminals — allowing payment in and out of an individual's account — would be installed in shops, petrol stations, hotels, airline companies, travel agents, British Rail, nationalised industries, council housing departments, large employers and so on. The entire financial life of an individual or family would be contained in a computerised account. Employers, through their computerised account, would transfer regular credits to their employees' accounts. To buy or order goods, the individual would present the equivalent of a credit card to the retailer: on a simple 'cash' sale, the computer would deduct the amount needed from the client's account and transfer it to the shop's account; on a 'credit' or hire purchase sale, the computer would inform the shop assistant whether or not the client was an acceptable credit risk and then accept instructions to debit the client's account each month for the amount of the credit each month. Other payments — a contribution to a political party, for instance — would similarly be transferred from one account to another.

In 1967, the Bank of Delaware at Wilmington in the United States was reported to be operating a pilot scheme, whereby customers of selected stores, who are also customers of the bank, make their purchases using plastic ID cards; the bank computer transfers the appropriate sum from the client's account into the store's.

Such a system would mean that an individual's entire financial life could become available to all the individuals involved in credit-checking, and operating financial transactions. It would be essential to build in procedures to protect the individual against snooping, for instance by programming a file with one or more codes to restrict entry to the computer file. But the possibilities for breach of confidentiality by the computer operators, or for unauthorised tapping via a remote terminal, remain staggering.

The Government would no doubt be quick to see the advantages which computerisation could provide. The Inland Revenue could, for instance, base its deduction on the computerised file. The Supplementary Benefits Commission could ensure that every individual entitled to benefit received it via the computer. Immediately, two Government departments would gain access to financial information about an individual's every transaction which would enable them to build up a detailed profile of each citizen — family relations; employment; sources of income; travel patterns; life-style; and political interests. Although, in theory, it would be possible to exclude the Inland Revenue from the system, it is hard to believe that Governments, having extended the powers of tax inspectors to enter people's homes and question their spouse and children, would resist the temptation to catch tax-dodgers via the computer. The most one could realistically hope for would be a requirement that tax inspectors would have to apply for a court search warrant, before invading an individual's data record. Thus the prospect opens up the Government and even its security services being linked in to the computerised file which would contain virtually every detail of the life of each one of us.

---

(1) *New Scientist,* 16 September 1976

(2) (1974) 3 W.L.R. 751

(3) See *Whose Conspiracy?,* Geoff Robertson, NCCL 1975 and *Conspiracy and Civil Liberties,* Robert Hazell, Papers in Social Administration, LSE 1975, for a full discussion of conspiracy law

(4) *Privacy Report,* Vol III No 5, December 1975, American Civil Liberties Union
(5) *Privacy Report,* III, 5
(6) *New Scientist,* 16 September 1976
(7) *Harvard Business Review,* March–April 197
(8) *Report of the Committee on Privacy,* Cmnd 5012, HMSO July 1972

Privacy and the media

NCCL has always stressed that privacy is not an absolute value, but one which must be balanced against other interests. The conflicting claims of privacy and press freedom are particularly hard to reconcile. There is considerable, and often well-founded, concern about some journalistic activities — the use of bugging devices, the activities of gossip columnists, or the pursuit of stories in a way which invades on people's private grief, for instance. But any attempt to legislate for privacy has been strongly resisted by the press on the grounds that privacy laws would restrict the investigation and exposure of matters of public concern.

In 1970, Justice published a draft privacy Bill, which would have enabled someone to sue in the civil courts for any substantial and unreasonable infringement of their privacy. But the Bill also provided for a complete defence where it could be shown that publication was in the public interest. When this Bill was introduced by Brian Walden MP, the press resisted it vigorously, and the Bill was withdrawn in return for the establishment of the Younger Committee.

In 1976, Harold Wilson, then Prime Minister, stated that the Government would be publishing a Green Paper on the laws of defamation and contempt, and the right to privacy, which would explore these issues in some detail. It is regrettable that the Green Paper has still not appeared. Shortly after the Prime Minister's speech, the Press Council published its declaration on individual privacy, which stated that the publication of information about someone's private life, without that person's consent, was only acceptable where there is a 'legitimate public interest overriding the right of privacy.' Even a public figure was entitled to respect for his or her privacy, except where circumstances relating to his private life could affect the performance of his duties or public confidence in him or his position. But they rejected proposals for a law on privacy on the grounds that the right to privacy could not be satisfactorily defined, and that legislation would be contrary to the public interest.

At the moment, someone who believes their privacy has been invaded by the media can make a complaint to the Press Council or the appropriate broadcasting authority. The Press Council's report will be published and a successful complainant will get an apology, but no compensation. An action for libel may be appropriate, but is only possible for someone rich enough to afford it. In most cases, the individual has no remedy.

In May 1976, ATV Today ran a programme on private detectives. To illustrate the ease with which private detectives can get information about people, ATV asked one detective to put together a dossier on Mr M. Mr M was selected by the programme researchers — and his name given to the detective, even though

> he had not been told about the programme or asked for his
> consent. On the programme, the detective held up the completed
> file, gave Mr M's name and said 'it seems he's still working in
> Birmingham and still working in the building industry. Obviously
> most of this information is confidential, but it does tell me how
> much he earns, and what debts he has.' The first Mr M knew about
> it was when he went to work the next day. Although Mr M says
> he got nowhere by his complaints to the studio, NCCL obtained
> an apology for him from ATV.

Alex Lyon MP, in his minority report on the Younger Committee, quoted a case to support his argument in favour of a right to privacy.

> 'I came across the case of a Mrs X whose policeman husband
> took a mistress. The wife prevailed upon him to give up the
> mistress and they were reconciled. The jealous lover told a
> national newspaper. When their reporter was rebuffed by Mrs X,
> they printed the story under the headline 'The Love Life of a
> Detective'. The family had to move; the husband had to give up
> his job; the child was teased at school. What do I now tell Mrs X?
> That the truth must prevail?'

NCCL remains convinced that a legal right to privacy is needed, but that there must be a strong 'public interest' defence which will ensure that the courts are directed towards the need to balance the conflicting claims of privacy and freedom of publication coming down in favour of press freedom wherever the invasion of privacy is justified in the public interest. It would be worth considering adapting for the law of defamation as well as a law of privacy the approach of the United States courts who drew the distinction (in the case of *Sullivan v. the New York Times*) between public officials and private individuals. A public official can only get damages for publication of a defamatory statement if he can prove that the statement was published maliciously — in other words, the journalist knew that it was untrue or negligently did not bother to find out whether it was true or not. But a private individual, someone who is unwillingly thrust into the limelight without having consented and without being involved in public affairs, should have legal redress against an unreasonable invasion of privacy.

This report has been concerned with one aspect of individual privacy — the right to know the contents of personal files and control their use. Information privacy is part of a wider issue — the right of the public to know about government operations and obtain information which governments keep secret without good cause. The right to know about government, and the right to know what government knows about you, are two sides of the same coin. A law to strengthen individual control of personal information, and a law to place the onus on government to justify the withholding of public information, would together make a decisive contribution towards redressing the balance of power in favour of the individual and the community, the governed, not the government. The issues are linked too in a different way: government secrecy conceals government invasions of privacy, and any opening up of government operations to public scrutiny will, amongst other things, reveal the extent to which personal information is collected, used and shared. The Official Secrets Acts prevent disclosure to the public of information to which the public have a right, and seriously inhibits press freedom. They should be replaced by a Freedom of Information law which, while protecting information whose publication would endanger national security and while ensuring that only the individual concerned and other authorised people would have access to the individual's personal records, would place a duty on government to make available other documents and information which are requested by members of the public or the press. NCCL is preparing a further report on 'the right to know' and the case for a freedom of information law.

A programme for action

The United Kingdom has fallen behind most Western countries in protecting individual privacy. We have already referred to privacy laws in the United States. In West Germany, a new Data Protection Act means that all personal data in computer data banks will have to be destroyed or permanently locked away after five years, and any company employing more than five people in automated data processing will have to appoint a 'data protection representative', directly responsible to the head of the organisation. The Act also means that a public register will be available of data banks. But the law, which comes into effect on 1 January 1978, contains a number of loopholes — most importantly that privacy measures are only required if the 'cost involved is reasonable in relation to the desired level of protection'. Allowing privacy protections to be dictated by cost is a sure way of having ineffective privacy safeguards.

France and the Netherlands both have new laws against unauthorised surveillance and the use of monitoring devices etc. The French Government has introduced a measure setting up a commission on computing and civil liberties; giving individuals the right to see their record (although only the commission itself can check a national security file) and prohibiting the computerisation of information on someone's ethnic origin or religious or political beliefs. Denmark has also introduced a new measure against unauthorised disclosure of information about another person's private affairs.

In Sweden, a Data Inspection Board has been established, with the responsibility of licensing all personal registers, in the private and public sectors, and supervising enforcement of a Data Act. In striking contrast to other European countries and to North America, Sweden has a highly automated and mainly centralised personal records system, combined with a long tradition of open access to government records. The Data Act provides that, before a licence can be given — and a data bank cannot operate without either a licence or Parliamentary authority — the Data Inspection Board must be satisfied that there is no reason to anticipate unauthorised infringements of someone's privacy. The Act also provides for people to be told about the contents of their personal records.

There is growing concern in Sweden about the vulnerability of computerised personal record systems to sabotage or external aggression, and a Ministry of Defense memorandum in 1976 stresses the need for new and more comprehensive security measures to protect the administration of society. The Swedish Government was the first to take action on the issue of transfer of personal information from one country to another. The revolution in international communications, including the development of satellite transmissions, makes it easy for information to be collected in one country, and coded, stored and re-transmitted in another. The fire brigade of

Malmo, Sweden, maintains a data bank of fire hazards in the town of 50,000 people. When the fire brigade is called out, the address is put into the computer terminal, which, a minute later, displays a list of any unusual hazards.
A standard use of a computer — but the computer is in Cleveland, Ohio.

Transferring information from one country to another makes it possible to evade the privacy controls of the country where the information was collected, and raises the prospect of 'data havens' — countries where privacy controls are weak or non-existent, and where companies or organisations unwilling to comply with privacy laws could transfer their computerised data. A few years ago, a German association of detective agencies, Intertect, grew worried about the proposed German data bank law and decided to transfer its data base to Luxembourg. The Swedish Data Act forbids the transfer of data for processing abroad, without a special license from the Data Inspectorate — and in 1975, the Inspectorate stopped information being exported to Britain, because British privacy laws are so inadequate. Proposed data laws in France and Holland also place special controls on the transfer of personal information.

International privacy standards are also being studied within the Council of Europe, the EEC and the Organisation for Economic Cooperation and Development. Moves towards common standards within, for example, the Common Market may help to put pressure on this country to introduce legislation of its own — although, at the same time, the absence of legislation in the UK may make the UK Government reluctant to agree to a Common Market directive.

British privacy law

British law is inadequate to protect privacy. Nothing has been done to implement the Younger Committee's recommendations on the use of bugging devices — the creation of a criminal offence of surreptitious surveillance by means of a technical device, and a civil wrong of surveillance (whether surreptitious or not) by means of a device. This would, for instance, cover telephone tapping — something which is only dealt with inadequately, if at all, by the present criminal law. Although the Wireless Telegraphy Acts require a licence for radio transmitters, it is rarely used against people who use bugs. The Theft Act 1968 makes it an offence to use electricity dishonestly, which would make it illegal to use a bug which drew power from telephone or electricity lines, but probably not one which had its own battery. Thus, any control of phone-tapping within the criminal law is uncertain and accidental, and was criticised as ineffective by both the Younger Committee and the Law Commission. Apart from private agents, the main users of phone taps are, of course, the Special Branch and security services, who are under a duty to obtain a warrant from the Home Secretary. But the Government has persistently refused to disclose the number of warrants issued each year.

Nor does British law adequately control other methods of obtaining information. On page 6, we showed how credit reference investigators who impersonated government officials to obtain information were convicted of conspiracy to effect a public mischief — an offence abolished by the House of Lords in 1974. The Law Commission has proposed a new criminal offence of obtaining confidential information by deception, and a civil action to cover the use or misuse of information unlawfully obtained. If both the Younger proposals and the Law Commission's suggestions were implemented — as NCCL believes they should be — someone could be prosecuted for obtaining confidential information by a bugging device or by deception, while the person who suffered by having information about his private life disclosed could sue for damages in the civil courts.

In the section on employment, we discussed the possible use of libel law as a way of dealing with inaccurate references. But an action for libel is not a satisfactory way of protecting the individual. Firstly, unless someone has a right to see the reference, it is unlikely that he or she will discover the source of the damage. Secondly, since references are protected by qualified privilege, someone suing for libel has to prove that the referee acted maliciously in giving an inaccurate reference. And since there is no legal aid available for libel actions, which have to be brought in the High Court, most people cannot afford even to make the attempt.

In theory, the law on breach of confidence could provide some protection for the individual who gives information, in confidence, to someone who then passes it on to a third party without the individual's consent. But in practice, as the Law Commission points out, the existing law is uncertain and confusing, and its potential as a protection for privacy has never been developed — partly because people whose privacy has been invaded often haven't suffered sufficient financial loss to risk the expenses of an uncertain court case. The Law Commission proposes that the law should be reformed, so that someone who provides confidential information could sue for damages in the civil courts if the recipient of the information communicated it without the giver's consent and caused the giver damage or distress as a result. The Law Commission suggest that it might be necessary to allow someone who broke a confidence to defend the action on the grounds of public interest or, at least, that it would be a defence to show that the information, although given in confidence, could be obtained from a public register or court report.

This suggested reform of the law on breach of confidence would provide more effective redress for someone whose privacy had been invaded. But it would not remove the need for a right to see and challenge personal files or, indeed, for a general legal right to privacy. Much of the information communicated about people is not information which they gave in confidence — it is information from other people, or deductions or opinions made by, for instance, a doctor or social worker. If a family is placed on a battered baby register partly because of information given by a neighbour, it is the neighbour who could sue the social services department for breach of confidence if they told the family the source of their information. While it may be necessary to protect anonymous informants, it is also necessary to protect the family — by giving them the right to know, and challenge, their inclusion in the register.

Apart from the Rehabilitation of Offenders Act, the only law specifically directed at protecting individual privacy is the Consumer Credit Act which, for the first time, gives the individual the right to see his or her record, and to challenge its contents, with the right to go to an independent body — the Director General of Fair Trading — should the credit reference agency refuse to make the required correction. As explained in the section on credit records, the Act has many defects, but it does at least embody the essential principle of individual access to the file — a principle which should be extended to other records held on the individual.

British law on privacy could be summarised like this:
- the use of most bugging devices and phone taps is not illegal;
- it is not a criminal offence to get confidential information by deception, or to release confidential information to someone who shouldn't have it;
- there is no right to bring an action for damages against invasion of privacy — except for libel or breach of confidence actions which are too expensive for most people, and unlikely to succeed anyway;
- except for credit reference files, there is no legal right for the individual to see the files kept on him or her;
- although the Rehabilitation of Offenders Act wipes out some convictions after a certain period, criminal records are still not secure against private agents or employers.

It is high time we caught up with other Western countries and introduced a comprehensive package of laws designed to protect people against the growing encroachment of government and private agencies.

The Government's proposals

The Government is committed to establishing a Data Protection Authority with responsibility for computerised data banks containing personal information. The White Paper in which this proposal is made[3] also sets out the principles which should govern the operation of data banks — that the existence and purpose of all data banks should be publicly known; that people should know what will happen to information they provide and that information given for one purpose should not be used for another without the person's consent or 'some other authorised justification'; that only necessary and relevant information should be stored and for no longer than is needed; and that statistics should not be published in a way which could identify individuals.

Welcome though the commitment to a Data Protection Authority and the statement of privacy principles are, the White Paper leaves much to be desired. It deals only with computers — although, as this report has stressed, the ordinary manilla file can contain as much irrelevant, inaccurate or unsubstantiated information as a computerised data bank. Under the Government's present proposals, manually-held systems — social security files, many medical and personnel records, files on pupils and students — would be left uncontrolled.

Secondly, the White Paper states that the privacy principles set out need not be enforced by either the criminal or civil law. So if irrelevant and inaccurate information is used about you or if confidential information given for one purpose is transferred, without your authority, to another department or agency, you cannot expect the law to support your right to privacy. You will have to take the complaint to the Data Protection Authority — for which the Government proposes two possible models. On the one hand, the Authority could be a registration and licensing agency, responsible for licensing data banks and ensuring that privacy safeguards were observed. On the other hand, the Authority could have the power to investigate complaints, get information about data banks, and make recommendations about them. If the second course is followed, the Authority would be left powerless to enforce its recommendations or take effective action to safeguard people's privacy; since the Ombudsman already has powers to investigate complaints of maladministration within the public sector, and make (unenforceable) recommendations, the Authority would add little to existing protection in the public sector and would be left, a toothless watchdog, guarding the private data banks only.

The White Paper quite rightly says that the most sensitive personal information is kept in medical records, criminal records, files held by the personal social services, employers and educational bodies, and records of people's financial position. But the Government also says that a number of data banks may need to be exempted from some of the privacy safeguards, especially the requirement that an individual should have a right to know what is in the file: some personnel records, on management grounds; information kept for the strict purposes of national security; information which facilitates the work of the police in preventing and detecting crime; medical records and possibly social work records. So, with the exception of financial and educational records, the most sensitive categories of information may end up being excluded, at least in part, from the Government's proposed privacy safeguards.

NCCL's proposals

NCCL is pressing for the following 10-point Charter of Fair Information Practice to be implemented. The Charter draws heavily on United States experience, but seeks to implement principles which have also been accepted in this country (by the Younger Committee and in the Government White Paper) as being fair and acceptable. Implementing the Charter would require a number of inter-related pieces of legislation, together with the establishment of a Data Protection Authority, independent of government, with the powers needed to supervise data banks, investigate complaints of invasions of privacy and, where necessary, bring legal action.

1. No personal data bank must be secret

You can't protect confidential information about yourself if you don't know who is collecting it. That is why the basic principle that there should be no data bank whose very existence is secret was stressed by the United States Department of Health, Education and Welfare in its Code of Fair Information Practice,4) and accepted by the UK Government in its White Paper. We propose that there should be a register of data banks, published and regularly up-dated by the new Data Protection Authority. The register should state: what the purpose of the data bank is; who is responsible for its maintenance; the statutory or other authority under which it was set up; the number of people covered; the type of information contained; the use to which the information is put; who has access to the information; and whether the individual can see and challenge his or her own file. The register should cover all systems — whether manual, mechanical or computerised — which contain personal information about identifiable individuals. Small systems could be exempt, although linked systems held by the same organisation, which together covered more than the minimum number of people, would be included.

2. Individuals should have the right to see, challenge and correct their own files.

The surest way of identifying any abuse of individual privacy, and removing inaccurate or irrelevant information, is to guarantee the individual the right to see his or her own file, challenge its accuracy, and ask for a correction or add a note of explanation or amendment to the file. Organisations which maintain personal records should be required to supply one copy of each file to the individual concerned at annual intervals, with additional copies being available on request and for a fee.

There will, of course, be some exceptions to this general right of access. NCCL supports the conclusion reached by the United States Federal Department of Health, Education and Welfare that only 'intelligence records', which presuppose the taking of adverse action against the individual and whose usefulness would be greatly reduced if their existence were revealed to the individual, should be exempt from legislation giving the individual the right to see the file. The Department concluded that 'any exception for a safeguard requirement that is proposed for any type of intelligence system must be specifically sanctioned by statute and then only if granting the exception would serve a societal interest that is clearly paramount to the interest served by having the requirement imposed.5)' These criteria would mean that individuals would not generally be able to see their police or national security files. There is no reason why someone shouldn't be allowed to check their criminal record. But *modus operandi* files on people with a criminal record, or current files on suspected terrorists, would come within the exemption. This does *not* mean, however, that police and national security files should continue to be maintained in the utmost secrecy. The existence of records held by C11, Special Branch and DI5, should be publicly admitted, together with the number of people covered. The new Authority should have the power to investigate complaints concerning these records.

3. There should be legal controls on the way in which information is collected

As we explained earlier in this section, there are virtually no legal controls on the way in which confidential information is collected — even if it involves bugging devices or the impersonation of government officials. We therefore support proposals for new criminal offences covering the surreptitious use of surveillance devices, and the obtaining of confidential information by deception. In addition, it should be grounds for disciplinary action or, in the most serious cases, dismissal for an employee deliberately to pass on confidential information about an individual to someone who is not authorised to receive it. We also propose that the power of government officials to obtain information by search warrants should be reviewed and restricted and that, except in emergencies, there should be no power of search without a court order.

The Younger Committee proposed a licensing system for private detectives who operate at present with no statutory controls at all. Although there are fears that licensing might give private detectives a spurious authority, NCCL believes that the advantages of overseeing private detectives' operations by a licensing authority outweigh the possible disadvantages. In 1977, Bruce George MP introduced a Private Member's Bill dealing with private detectives and security firms, and this Bill provides an excellent model for legislation.

Much information, of course, is collected directly from the individual. Any request for information should state precisely under what authority the information is requested; whether it is compulsory to answer; what the consequences are of a refusal to answer; where the information will be stored; how it will be used, and who will have access to it. A vehicle registration form would, therefore, carry a statement explaining, amongst other things, that the information would be stored in the Swansea Vehicle Registration Index and transferred to the National Police Computer, the Home Office, the Inland Revenue, other Government departments and local authorities.

4. Information collected should be relevant and should be the minimum needed

Privacy legislation should state that information collected on an individual should be 'relevant and necessary' to the licensed purpose of the data bank. The new Authority should be given the job of drawing up detailed guidelines for different data banks, stressing the need to avoid recording in a central system personal opinions on an individual, particularly where these are cast in pseudo-scientific form (terms such as 'paranoid' or 'neurotic' should never be used by lay people to record their own judgment on someone). No system should be allowed to store information about someone's politics, religion or sexual activity, unless the organisation involved is authorised to collect such information for the direct purpose of enforcing the criminal law. Time limits should also be prescribed, since information which was relevant when it was new may be quite irrelevant five years later. The West German law provides for information to be destroyed or locked away after five years: we would support a single time limit of this nature, which ensures the regular destruction or up-dating of information.

Where information is being gathered for statistical purposes, survey forms should, if possible, not contain the name or address of the individual interviewed. Where identifying information is needed for the duration of the survey, it should be destroyed as soon as the details are transferred to the data bank, or maintained only in the form of an index, linking the identifying details of an individual by a number to the other answers to the survey form.

5. Information given for one purpose should not be used for another without the individual's knowledge and consent

It is not enough to demand the right to see personal files, and correct the information stored there, if the information continues to be transferred to other people without legal or other controls. We therefore propose that, as a basic rule, any information system should need to ask the individual's consent to further use of the information, either at the time the individual gives the information or when the proposal to transfer it to a third party is made. If the transfer is made under Parliamentary authority, this must be made clear in the register of data banks and in any request or demand for personal information. Of course, some limited consent to communication of personal information is implied when information is given: patients presumably realise that some of what they tell the doctor will be shared with a secretary, although they have a right to expect the secretary to be bound by the same rules of confidentiality as the doctor. But the patient should be told about, and asked to consent to, any further transfer of information, whether to the DHSS or Regional Health Authority computers or to the local authority social services department. Control on the use of personal information means rethinking the legal definitions of who owns the information. Patient consent to transfer of medical data cannot be enforced as long as the DHSS owns the GP's notes.

Finally, any data bank licensed by the DPA should be required to keep a 'log' of who requests and is given access to an individual's record. Such a log can be used to protect security in a computerised file, by alerting the computer operator to an unauthorised request. It also provides a means for the person in charge of the system, the individual concerned, or the DPA when investigating a complaint, to find out whether transfers of information have been properly controlled.

6. There must be legal restrictions on the linkage of personal record systems

The public is right to fear the prospect of a marriage between the different systems which keep personal information on people. Highly confidential information which is given for one purpose — for instance, in the course of medical or psychiatric treatment — is safe when it is only communicated to the doctor or psychiatrist. In the hands of a national government computer, it is not. The Government has pledged that no linkage of the different government data banks is planned: this pledge should be backed by a legal ban on the creation of a single national data bank. Any future Government which tried to change the law would have to publicise its plans, and might well fail to get Parliamentary agreement.

Falling short of the complete linkage of different systems is the increasing transfer of information from one system to another — for instance, from the Swansea Vehicle Register to other government departments and local authorities. Any such transfers must be publicised, and should only be made with the consent of the individual or, when there is an over-riding public interest, Parliament.

7. Transfer of personal information abroad must be controlled

If the United Kingdom were to legislate for tough privacy controls, on the lines proposed here, some agencies might try to avoid the consequences by transferring their computerised data banks to a country without equivalent controls. The Data Protection Act should forbid the transfer of personal information without the consent of the new Authority, which should be under a duty only to consent to such a transfer when it was satisfied that the information stored abroad would be subject to the same safeguards as that stored here.

8. Codes of practice should be developed for all those involved in collecting and storing personal information

The computer industry has begun to develop professional codes for computer operators, in order to set proper standards, backed by professional sanctions, for confidentiality and security. The British Association of Social Workers has published a Code of Ethics for its members, which places considerable emphasis on the need to respect confidentiality. NALGO at its 1977 Annual Conference passed a resolution calling on its national executive committee to develop a code of practice for local government and health service workers, in order to protect the individual's right to privacy. The new Data Protection Authority could play a most useful role in helping to formulate such codes of practice with the different groups of workers who are responsible for ensuring individual privacy.

9. The law should guarantee the individual's right to privacy

Although the specific proposals mentioned above to control the collection, use and transfer of personal information, would do a great deal towards protecting people's privacy, NCCL believes that a general legal right of privacy remains essential, allowing individuals to bring a civil action for damages (and, where appropriate, an injunction) where their privacy had been invaded. It is impossible to foresee the full impact of technological development on individual privacy, or for Acts of Parliament to keep up with the controls which will be needed. A general right of privacy, combined with the other legal and administrative safeguards just proposed, would ensure that those whose privacy had been invaded would have a legal remedy. As suggested in the section on the media, it should be a defence to a privacy action to show that publication was justified in the public interest and consideration should be given to treating public figures differently from private individuals.

10. A Data Protection Authority should be established to supervise collection and storage of personal information

The Government has committed itself to setting up a Data Protection Authority, responsible for computerised data banks. NCCL believes it is essential to extend the Authority's brief to include non-computerised data banks. Although computers dramatically change the scale on which information can be stored and used, this report has shown that manual systems can also represent a threat to the individual. Indeed, a law which controlled computerised systems only could even encourage agencies to transfer their information to manual systems, in order to evade privacy controls altogether. The Authority should be able to enforce the requirement that an individual should have access to his or her record and the right to challenge and correct its contents, in the same way that the Director General of Fair Trading can enforce the provisions of the Consumer Credit Act. An operator who cannot guarantee privacy safeguards, or who refuses to comply with the law, would risk being refused a licence or having a licence taken away. There should be a right of appeal against refusal or withdrawal of a licence by the Authority, either to a court or to a Data Bank Tribunal.

---

(1) Breach of Confidence, Law Commission Working Paper No 58, HMSO 1974

If you are asked to provide information about yourself - or about someone else - *ask:*

>Why do they want it?
>Is the information really necessary?
>Is there a law which says you have to give the information?
>Who will store the information, and for how long?
>Who will be able to see the information?
>Will you (or the person on whom the information is kept) be able to see the file and challenge its accuracy, if necessary?

If you're not satisfied with the answers, and if there is no legal requirement that you give the information, consider whether you should give it at all. Take the matter up with your MP, local authority, with your Member of Parliament or local councillor, or the Government Department or local authority which is collecting the information.

NCCL will be happy to send you, free, more information about the right to privacy. An order form is on the next page.

The National Council for Civil Liberties has campaigned since 1934 to defend and extend freedom of speech and expression, and to protect the rights of individuals and minorities to equal treatment under just laws. NCCL advises people on their rights; takes cases to courts and tribunals; lobbies Parliament and Government through an all-party Parliamentary Civil Liberties Group; publishes pamphlets about people's rights; and organises campaigns for law reforms. Recent campaigns have centred on wrongful conviction of innocent people; the need for an independent police complaints authority; women's rights; and the need for fairer nationality and immigration laws. Funded solely by subscriptions and donations, NCCL is the largest independent organisation working for human rights in the United Kingdom.

NCCL's 'right to know' campaign was launched in 1977, to campaign against secret government, and to press for a new law on individual privacy and the right for individuals to see and challenge secret personal files. **We urgently need your help in this campaign.** You can use the form below to get more information about NCCL and the campaign.

NAME ....

ADDRESS ....

....

Please send me ...... copy(ies) of *Privacy: The Information Gatherers*, at £1.25 each, post included.

Please send me ...... free leaflet(s) on the privacy campaign.

Please send me ...... free leaflet(s) on people's rights to see their credit reference files.

Please send me more information about NCCL. (   )

I enclose a donation of £   .   towards your 'right to know' campaign.

Please return this form to NCCL 'Right to Know' Campaign, 186 Kings Cross Road, London WC1X 9DE.